Annual Update

2013

US Government & Politics

Anthony J. Benne

Philip Allan, an imprint of Hodder Education, an Hachette UK company, Market Place, Deddington, Oxfordshire OX15 0SE

Orders

Bookpoint Ltd, 130 Milton Park, Abingdon, Oxfordshire OX14 4SB

tel: 01235 827827

fax: 01235 400401

e-mail: education@bookpoint.co.uk

Lines are open 9.00 a.m.–5.00 p.m., Monday to Saturday, with a 24-hour message answering service. You can also order through the Philip Allan website: www.philipallan.co.uk

© Anthony J. Bennett 2013

ISBN 978-1-4441-6890-7

First printed 2013

Impression number 5 4 3 2 1

Year 2016 2015 2014 2013

Typeset by Integra Software Services Pvt. Ltd., Pondicherry, India

Printed by CPI Group (UK) Ltd, Croydon, CR0 4YY

Hachette UK's policy is to use papers that are natural, renewable and recyclable products and made from wood grown in sustainable forests. The logging and manufacturing processes are expected to conform to the environmental regulations of the country of origin.

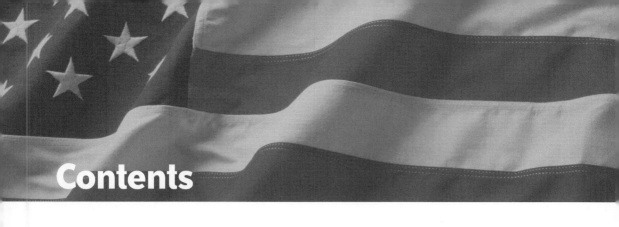

Contents

Chapter 1

The not-so-invisible 'invisible primary'

What you need to know

- The invisible primary is the term used to refer to the events in the year prior to a presidential election, before the actual primaries and caucuses begin.
- It is called 'invisible' because, traditionally, events that occurred during this period could not actually be seen. They occurred mostly behind the scenes, out of the eye of the media.
- The important things that a would-be candidate needs to concentrate on during this period are increasing name recognition, raising money and putting together the necessary state-based organisation.
- The media now play an increasingly important role during this period by staging intra-party televised debates between the would-be candidates.
- The candidate leading in opinion polls at the end of the invisible primary often goes on to become that party's presidential nominee, thus enhancing the importance of the invisible primary.

Setting the scene

The election of 2012 — like those of 1984, 1992, 1996 and 2004 — featured a president running for re-election. This always gives the race a different character from those in which no incumbent is running — those, for example, of 2000 and 2008. For a start, the incumbent president usually — though not always — gains the nomination of his own party without any serious competition. That was the case for Ronald Reagan in 1984, Bill Clinton in 1996 and George W. Bush in 2004, though not for George H. W. Bush in 1992. In 2012, President Obama did not have to fight for re-nomination. That put him at an immediate advantage for he could save all his hard-raised cash for the general election campaign, spending hardly a cent in the primaries where he was virtually unopposed.

It is no coincidence that historically incumbent presidents who are not challenged for their own party's nomination go on to win in November, while those who do have to fight for re-nomination — President Ford in 1976, President Carter in 1980 and President Bush in 1992 — all went on to lose in the general election. So the first effect President Obama's running for re-election had on the 2012 election was that all the attention in the primaries was on the Republicans.

Table 1.1 Presidents losing re-election bid

Presidents losing re-election bid	Date
John Quincy Adams	1828
Martin Van Buren	1840
Grover Cleveland	1888
Benjamin Harrison	1892
William Howard Taft	1912
Herbert Hoover	1932
Gerald Ford	1976
Jimmy Carter	1980
George H. W. Bush	1992

The second effect an incumbent president often has on the race is a shorter than usual list of candidates for the challenging party. It is a simple historical fact that presidents usually win a second term. Between 1796 and 2004, 30 presidents ran for re-election of whom 21 won and just 9 lost, with Ford, Carter and the first Bush being the only presidential losers in the last 75 years (Table 1.1). Because the odds are stacked against a win by the challenging party, some prospective top-tier candidates may decide to sit out the race, waiting for a more propitious election cycle — perhaps in 4 years' time.

The Republican candidates

Table 1.2 lists the eight Republicans who announced that they would not be running in 2012. Most of these would have aspired to be top-tier candidates had they decided to run. Four incumbent governors — Bobby Jindal of Louisiana, Haley Barbour of Mississippi, Mitch Daniels of Indiana and Chris Christie of New Jersey — all announced their non-candidacies. 'I'm not running for president in 2012, period,' stated Governor Jindal nearly 2 years before the election. 'I will not be a candidate for president next year,' announced Governor Barbour in April 2011. 'Now is not my time,' stated Governor Christie after a late surge to draft him seemed to be gathering momentum late in 2011.

But even without the eight potential candidates listed in Table 1.2, there were plenty of would-be Republican candidates ready to throw their hats into the ring. Of the dozen names listed in Table 1.3 there were probably only four who seemed to qualify as potentially top-tier candidates.

Newt Gingrich was a former speaker of the House of Representatives and had been largely responsible for the stunning victory of his party in the congressional mid-term elections back in 1994. But Gingrich always courted controversy whether in his private or political life. At 51, Tim Pawlenty had just completed two terms as governor of Minnesota and was highly regarded as an astute politician. It was therefore something of a surprise that his candidacy lasted less than 3 months, being the first to exit the field over 4 months before voting began in the primaries and

Table 1.2 Republicans who announced their non-candidacies

Name	Date announced not running
Governor Bobby Jindal	16 November **2010**
Senator John Thune	22 February **2011**
Governor Haley Barbour	25 April
Ex-Governor Mike Huckabee	14 May
Donald Trump	16 May
Governor Mitch Daniels	22 May
Governor Chris Christie	4 October
Ex-Governor Sarah Palin	5 October

Table 1.3 Republican candidates: dates entering and leaving the race

Name	Date announced candidacy (2011)	Date ended bid
Ex-Governor Gary Johnson	21 April	28 December 2011*
Ex-Rep. Newt Gingrich	11 May	2 May 2012
Rep. Ron Paul	13 May	14 May 2012
Herman Cain	21 May	3 December 2011
Ex-Governor Tim Pawlenty	23 May	14 August 2011
Ex-Governor Mitt Romney	2 June	[eventual nominee]
Ex-Senator Rick Santorum	6 June	10 April 2012
Rep. Michele Bachmann	13 June	4 January 2012
Ex-Governor Jon Huntsman	21 June	16 January 2012
Rep. Thaddeus McCotter	2 July	22 September 2011
Ex-Governor Buddy Roemer	21 July	22 February 2012
Governor Rick Perry	13 August	19 January 2012

* became Libertarian Party presidential candidate

caucuses. Governor Rick Perry of Texas was another Republican whose candidacy virtually crash landed on take-off. The last entrant into the race, Perry lasted a mere 5 months before bowing to the inevitable. And then there was Mitt Romney.

It seemed relatively inconceivable that any of the other eight names would end up as the Republicans' presidential candidate of 2012, though that's not to say that even no-hopers such as Herman Cain, Ron Paul and Michele Bachmann did not have their 15 minutes of fame as the contest wound its weary way from debate to debate through the latter half of 2011.

The invisible primary

The so-called invisible primary is the period before the voting begins in the primaries and caucuses. In terms of dates it is therefore pretty much synonymous with the calendar year before the election year — 2011 in this case. When the

term was coined back in the 1970s it was said to be 'invisible' because there was nothing much to see, though that is less true nowadays. The main features of this period have always been:

- official declaration of candidacies — or non-candidacies
- fundraising
- putting together the necessary organisation, especially in those states holding early or key caucuses/primaries
- increasing name recognition

In recent election cycles there have been a series of televised debates in which the candidates of one party take part. In 2007, as both parties were seeking to nominate a new candidate, there were both Democratic and Republican debates. But in 2011 there were only debates between the would-be Republican candidates. These debates have become more numerous and potentially more important in each successive election cycle. They also make the term 'invisible primary' rather inappropriate as there is now much — some would say, too much — to see during this period of the pre-nomination cycle.

Table 1.4 shows the schedule of 15 Republican debates which were held before a single vote was cast in any state caucus or primary. Most were held in those states holding the key early primaries and caucuses — Iowa (4), New Hampshire (2), South Carolina (2) and Florida (2). Five of the debates were sponsored by the conservative cable television station Fox News, with CNN sponsoring four.

Table 1.4 Republican candidate debates held before the Iowa caucuses

Date (2011)	Sponsor	Venue	Number of candidates participating
5 May	Fox News	Greenville, South Carolina	5
13 June	CNN	Manchester, New Hampshire	7
11 August	Fox News	Ames, Iowa	8
7 September	NBC News	Reagan Library, California	8
12 September	CNN	Tampa, Florida	8
22 September	Fox News	Orlando, Florida	9
11 October	Washington Post	Hanover, New Hampshire	8
18 October	CNN	Las Vegas, Nevada	7
9 November	CNBC	Rochester, Michigan	8
12 November	CBS News	Spartanburg, South Carolina	8
19 November	The Family Leader	Des Moines, Iowa	6
22 November	CNN	Washington DC	8
3 December	Fox News	New York City	6
10 December	ABC News	Des Moines, Iowa	6
15 December	Fox News	Sioux City, Iowa	7

Table 1.5 Poll leaders in Real Clear Politics poll of polls, August to December 2011

Date (2011)	Poll leader	Percentage
15 August	Mitt Romney	19.6
12 September	Rick Perry	31.8
9 October	Mitt Romney	21.8
10 November	Herman Cain	25.2
10 December	Newt Gingrich	33.3

The hallmark of the Republican nomination contest was the number of candidates who led the field in the seemingly endless cycle of opinion polls. Taking the poll of polls as put together by the website Real Clear Politics (**www.realclearpolitics.com**) the lead changed five times in the last 5 months of 2011 (Table 1.5) — and it changed another five times during the first 2 months of 2012. Seven different candidates — Romney, Bachmann, Perry, Cain, Gingrich, Paul and Santorum — led the field in the 6 months between August 2011 and February 2012 as Republicans seemed to be searching desperately for a truly conservative candidate to put up against President Obama. It seemed that the Republican rank and file wanted anyone but Romney.

The first to emerge as the not-the-Romney candidate was the unlikely figure of Michele Bachmann, the House member from Minnesota's 6th Congressional District, a true conservative, Tea Party favourite and evangelical Christian. Ms Bachmann shot to prominence by winning the Ames Straw Poll in Iowa on 13 August 2011 — now a traditional event in the Republican Party's invisible primary calendar. But the Bachmann bubble soon burst and she quit the race immediately after her sixth place finish in the Iowa caucuses in January 2012.

One evening in Rochester

With Bachmann's star quickly fading, it was Rick Perry who emerged in October as the rising star in the Republican contest. But Perry fell foul of the televised debates in which his halting performances were a significant impediment. It was in the ninth of these debates, in Rochester, Michigan, on 9 November, that Governor Perry hit the rocks. Here is how Perry's debate — and campaign — fell apart in conversation with panellist John Harwood of CNBC:

RICK PERRY: And I'll tell you, it's three agencies of government when I get [to Washington] that are gone, Commerce, Education and the — what's the third one there? Let's see. [Audience laughter]

RON PAUL: You need five.

PERRY: Oh, five, OK.

PAUL: Yes.

PERRY: So Commerce, Education, and the —

VOICE OFF: EPA? [Environmental Protection Agency]

PERRY: EPA, there you go. No. [Laughter. Cheering and applause]

HARWOOD: Seriously, is the EPA the one you were talking about?

PERRY: No, Sir. No, Sir. We were talking about the agencies of government I would do away with, the Education, the —

VOICE OFF: Commerce.

PERRY: Commerce, and let's see. I can't. The third one. Sorry. Oops.

It was painful to watch. Most human beings felt for Perry as they had done for other high-profile politicians who had either been embarrassed or embarrassed themselves in the public arena of a televised debate. But moments like this are much more significant when they reinforce previously held views of the candidate. Back in 1984, the great communicator Ronald Reagan could stumble and blather through a 90-minute debate with his opponent Walter Mondale and still go on to win 49 states less than a month later. But here's how PBS *News Hour*'s political editor David Chalian saw things the following day when asked how much damage had been done to the Perry campaign:

> Well, I think, if it were any other candidate, the damage might be limited, because everybody can understand having a total mental lapse like that. We have all been in positions like that. The problem for Rick Perry is that a moment like that feeds into a larger narrative about his campaign. The debates have been a major trouble spot for him. From the moment he got into the race, he has looked unprepared and unable to debate his competitors on the stage. This was by far the worst flub he had. And that just feeds into the notion that he's not ready for prime time.

Perry had shot from late-starter in August to poll leader by mid-September, but his campaign was already faltering before he failed to recall the name of the Department of Energy — that elusive third agency of government which he had wanted to abolish. His campaign never recovered.

But it was quickly forgotten that the same debate in Rochester had a second memorable moment — one which worked to the advantage of another of the 'Stop Romney' candidates. Herman Cain's campaign was also floundering in early November over accusations of sexual harassment when he was CEO of Godfather's Pizza. Another of the press panellists that evening, Maria Bartiromo, launched into a question about this:

> Mr Cain, the American people want jobs, but they also want leadership. They want character in a president. In recent days, we have learned that four women have accused you of inappropriate behaviour. Here, we're focusing on character and judgement.

At that point, a number of members of the audience started to boo, clearly unhappy with Ms Bartiromo's line of questioning. In contrast, Mr Cain's robust defence of himself was greeted with cheering and prolonged applause. This illustrates another rule of thumb: Republican candidates can gain support by portraying themselves as victims of the 'liberal media'. By the next morning, Cain was leading many Republican polls. In the previous 6 weeks, he had raised $9 million — and $2.5 million of that had come in since the allegations were first reported in the media. Victim Cain left Rochester that night a happy man — but a vulnerable one too. As more women made more allegations, Cain was eventually forced into a humiliating climb down and was out of the race less than a month after that Rochester debate.

Romney was not so much defeating his opponents by force of argument as merely waiting for them to self-destruct: first Bachmann, then Perry, now Cain. Next in line would be the former House Speaker Newt Gingrich. If Bachmann, Perry and Cain were mere undergraduates of the school of self-destruction, Gingrich could claim to already have a PhD from the same institution. But this was the time for Gingrich's moments in the sunshine. We would have to wait until later for Gingrich to topple — again.

A lack of clarity

In previous nomination cycles, the invisible primary has clarified the Republican race and the frontrunner at the end of the year preceding the election has almost always gone on to win the nomination. But the invisible primary of 2011 did little if anything to clarify the Republican race. It seemed like Mitt Romney was the strongest candidate and with a field as weak as this one, he should have seen off his opponents as easily as George W. Bush had done in 1999–2000 or Bob Dole in 1995–96. But rank and file Republicans had a number of reservations about the former Massachusetts governor — that he was too liberal, that he was too elitist, that he was a flip-flopper, that he was an uninspiring campaigner and orator — and many were wary of his Mormon religion. If they were not careful, they would be writing the Democrats' script for them. Thus the calendar year 2011 ended with no consistent Republican frontrunner. There was therefore all to play for as the Republicans of Iowa attended their party caucuses on the evening of 3 January 2012.

Questions

1 What was significant about the fact that President Obama faced no significant opposition in the Democratic primaries in 2012?
2 What is the record of incumbent presidents being re-elected?
3 Name four potentially top-tier Republican candidates who did not enter the 2012 presidential race.
4 What are the main features of the invisible primary?
5 Why is the term 'invisible primary' rather inappropriate nowadays?
6 How and why did the Republican candidate debate on 9 November affect the nomination race?
7 Why, according to David Chalian, did Governor Perry's 'flub' have such a significant effect on the future of his campaign?
8 What concerns did many Republican voters have about Mitt Romney?

Chapter 2

The 2012 primaries: mainly about Romney

What you need to know

- Presidential primaries are state-based elections held between January and June of the presidential election year.
- They give ordinary voters a chance to say who they would like to be their party's candidate in the upcoming presidential election.
- Voters in the primaries also choose delegates to go to the national party conventions held in late summer, which is where the final decision about the candidate is made.
- Some small, sparsely-populated states hold caucuses rather than a primary.
- Caucuses are a series of meetings held across the state which perform the same functions as primaries.

Changing the rules

As explained in Chapter 1, the 2012 primaries were an almost exclusively Republican affair because President Obama received no significant opposition in claiming re-nomination by the Democratic Party. Ever since the rules for selecting presidential candidates and national convention delegates were radically reformed as a result of the McGovern–Fraser Commission in the early 1970s, both major parties have tinkered with the rules before each new election cycle.

Ahead of the 2012 nomination race, the Republican Temporary Delegate Selection Committee made certain recommendations that were adopted by the Republican National Committee (RNC). First, it pushed back the potential start date of the contest. The RNC rules called for Iowa, New Hampshire, Nevada and South Carolina to be allowed to hold their contests in February, but all the other states were to keep to a window between 6 March and 12 June. Second, it forbade any Republican state party from staging a winner-takes-all contest before 1 April.

But not all the RNC plan was implemented. State parties guard their autonomy jealously and the 2012 nomination season in the end opened on exactly the same date as it did in 2008. Once Florida and South Carolina had announced they were ignoring the RNC rules by scheduling their primaries in late January, Iowa and New Hampshire, who by tradition hold the first-in-the-nation caucuses and primary, leapfrogged them to schedule their contests in early January. Arizona and Michigan broke the rules too by scheduling their contests in February. This resulted in a penalty of a 50% reduction in national convention delegate allocation for New Hampshire, South Carolina, Florida, Arizona and Michigan. Iowa avoided the penalty by turning its caucuses into a 'non-binding' contest, meaning that no convention delegates were allocated as a result of the vote on 3 January. Allocation came later at a state party convention held in June. Colorado, Minnesota, Missouri and Maine also avoided a penalty by holding non-binding contests.

There were two breaches of the winner-takes-all rule when Florida and Arizona both scheduled winner-takes-all primaries before 1 April. But as both state parties had already lost 50% of their delegate allocation for breaching the 6 March window, the RNC decided not to impose any further punishments. But these states clearly believed that scheduling their contests early and/or holding a winner-takes-all contest was more beneficial in enhancing their status in the nomination contest than gaining a few more delegates at the convention in August. This shows the relative importance of primaries vis-à-vis the conventions.

The result of these rule changes was to elongate the nomination contest, moving away from the stampede towards 'front loading' which had been a feature of nomination cycles for over 20 years. Super Tuesday, which saw 21 Republican contests on 6 February in 2008, featured just 10 Republican contests and occurred a month later in 2012. Some large states with large numbers of delegates at stake moved their contests to later in the cycle: New York moved from 5 February (2008) to 24 April (2012); California from 5 February (2008) to 5 June (2012). The thirty-seventh Republican contest which occurred on 19 February in 2008 occurred on 24 April in 2012. The number of winner-takes-all primaries fell from seventeen in 2008 to just eight in 2012. As we shall see, this meant that it was going to take much longer to amass the necessary number of delegates to win the nomination than in previous nomination cycles.

The Iowa caucuses

Ever since Democrat Jimmy Carter scored an upset victory in the Iowa Democratic caucuses back in 1976, the myth of presidential politics has been that 'the road to the presidential nomination — even to the White House — lies through Iowa'. Yet in the Republican Party, Ronald Reagan lost the Iowa caucuses in 1980, as did George H. W. Bush in 1988 and John McCain in 2008. All three went on to win their party's presidential nomination that year and two of them — Reagan and Bush — went on to win the White House. The race of 2012 was to be the fourth out of the last six competitively-contested Iowa Republican caucuses which the eventual presidential nominee failed to win (Table 2.1).

This was also the second nomination cycle in a row when the Ames Straw Poll, the Iowa Republican caucuses and the Republican presidential nomination were won by three different candidates, again calling into question the role of Iowa in identifying the party's presidential nominee. In 2007–08, the Ames Straw Poll winner was Mitt Romney, with the Iowa caucuses being won by Mike Huckabee, but the eventual nominee was John McCain. In August 2011, Michele

Table 2.1 Result of Iowa Republican caucuses, 2012

Candidate	Votes	Percentage
Rick Santorum	29,839	24.56
Mitt Romney	29,805	24.53
Ron Paul	26,036	21.43
Newt Gingrich	16,163	13.30
Rick Perry	12,557	10.33
Michele Bachmann	6,046	4.98
Jon Huntsman	739	0.61

Bachmann had won the Ames Straw Poll, but in the caucuses on 3 January 2012, she came a distant sixth with just under 5% of the vote. Determining and announcing the winner of the contest was something of a muddle. The media initially reported that Mitt Romney had won the contest by just eight votes. But nearly 3 weeks later, the Iowa Republican Party released the certified results which showed that the former Pennsylvania senator, Rick Santorum, had won the caucuses by 34 votes.

The key to success in these early caucus and primary states is in exceeding expectations and the Iowa Republican caucuses of 2012 were a prime example of this for both Romney and Santorum. For Romney, a second place finish — even just 0.03 percentage points behind the winner — was a disappointment. Romney, with Republican establishment backing, money, name recognition and national frontrunner status, needed to win in Iowa just to live up to the expectations of his candidacy. By contrast, Santorum had spent most of 2011 struggling even to stay in the race. Even in Iowa, as recently as mid-December, his poll numbers were in the low single digits and he could afford only a pick-up truck to travel round the state. But suddenly, as conservative voters drifted away from Bachmann, Cain, Gingrich and Perry, and a last-minute write-in campaign on behalf of Sarah Palin failed to get off the ground, Santorum became the flavour of the month. A third place finish would have been marvellous. Victory was a sensation and greatly increased Santorum's money raising potential while raising him to top-tier status among the remaining candidates.

The groups of voters among which Santorum gained his strongest support were instructive. He won his strongest support among:
- those for whom abortion was the most important issue (58%)
- 45–64 year olds (36%)
- very conservative voters (35%)
- evangelical Christians (32%)

But when caucus-goers were asked to identify the most important candidate quality, top of the poll was 'Can defeat Obama' named by 31%, and among that group Romney beat Santorum by 48% to just 13%.

Three more contests in January

In what became a hallmark of this nomination race, Santorum's moment in the spotlight soon passed. Romney's easy victory in New Hampshire soon became the new media talking point. Santorum, meanwhile, finished a poor fourth in New Hampshire, followed by a distant third in both South Carolina and Florida, failing to reach 20% in any of these three contests (Table 2.2). It was time for another comeback by former House Speaker Newt Gingrich who once again became the new conservative favourite.

Table 2.2 Republican primary and caucus results, 2012

Date	State	Romney (%)	Santorum (%)	Gingrich (%)	Paul (%)
3 Jan	Iowa (C)	25	**25**	13	21
10 Jan	New Hampshire	**39**	9	9	23
21 Jan	South Carolina	28	17	**40**	13
31 Jan	*Florida*	**46**	13	32	7
4 Feb	Nevada (C)	**50**	10	21	19
7 Feb	Colorado (C)	35	**40**	13	12
	Minnesota (C)	17	**45**	11	27
	Missouri	25	**55**	–	12
11 Feb	Maine (C)	**39**	18	6	36
28 Feb	*Arizona*	**47**	27	16	8
	Michigan	**41**	38	7	12
9–29 Feb	Wyoming (C)	**44**	27	–	12
3 Mar	Washington (C)	**38**	24	10	25
6 Mar	Alaska (C)	**32**	29	14	24
(Super	Georgia	26	20	**47**	7
Tuesday)	Idaho (C)	**62**	18	2	18
	Massachusetts	**72**	12	5	10
	North Dakota (C)	24	**40**	8	28
	Ohio	**38**	37	15	9
	Oklahoma	28	**34**	28	10
	Tennessee	28	**37**	24	9
	Vermont	**40**	24	8	26
	Virginia	**60**	–	–	40
10 Mar	Kansas (C)	21	**51**	14	13
13 Mar	Alabama	29	**35**	29	5
	Hawaii (C)	**45**	25	11	19
	Mississippi	31	**33**	31	4
20 Mar	Illinois	**47**	35	8	9

(Continued)

Table 2.2 Republican primary and caucus results, 2012 (Continued)

Date	State	Romney (%)	Santorum (%)	Gingrich (%)	Paul (%)
24 Mar	Louisiana	27	**49**	16	6
3 Apr	*District of Columbia*	70	–	11	12
	Maryland	49	29	11	10
	Wisconsin	44	37	6	11
24 Apr	Connecticut	67	7	10	13
	Delaware	56	6	27	11
	New York	62	9	13	16
	Pennsylvania	58	18	10	13
	Rhode Island	63	5	6	24
8 May	Indiana	65	13	6	16
	North Carolina	66	10	8	11
	West Virginia	70	12	6	11
15 May	Nebraska	71	14	5	10
	Oregon	72	9	6	12
22 May	Arkansas	68	13	5	13
	Kentucky	67	9	6	13
29 May	Texas	69	8	5	12
5 June	California	80	5	4	10
	Montana	68	9	4	14
	New Jersey	81	5	3	10
	New Mexico	73	11	6	10
	South Dakota	66	11	4	13
26 June	*Utah*	93	2	0	5
Number of contests won		**38**	**11**	**2**	**0**

(C): Caucuses
Bold italics = winner-take-all contest
Bold = winner

Gingrich's January resurrection was another example of the influence of the televised debates which had sunk Rick Perry and temporarily boosted Herman Cain during the invisible primary (see Chapter 1). As Republicans began to take another look at Gingrich, the media were carrying more stories of his matrimonial difficulties, specifically allegations of infidelity made by Gingrich's second wife, Marianne. In a debate in South Carolina just 3 days before that state's Republican primary, CNN's John King opened the debate thus:

> Just as [former] Speaker Gingrich surged into contention here in South Carolina
> a direct fresh character attack on the Speaker. And Mr Speaker, I want to start

with that this evening. As you know, your ex-wife gave an interview to ABC News and another to the *Washington Post,* and this story has now gone viral on the Internet. In it, she says that you came to her in 1999, at a time when you were having an affair. She says you asked her to enter into an 'open marriage.' Would you like to take some time to respond to that?

Gingrich's immediate response was short, angry — but brilliant. 'No — but I will.' There was instant, loud and prolonged applause from a significant section of the debate audience. Gingrich continued:

> I think the destructive, vicious, negative nature of much of the news media makes it harder to govern this country, harder to attract decent people to run for public office. And I am appalled that you would begin a presidential debate on a topic like that.

By now, the Gingrich supporters were on their feet, whooping and whistling. King, who at the outset had stridden onto the stage in front of the candidates to launch his verbal missile, now looked a rather isolated and slightly embarrassed figure. 'Is that all you want to say, sir?' enquired King — more in hope than expectation. But Gingrich, with the audience clearly behind him, was not going to pass up such a golden opportunity to lambast the 'despicable' media. 'Let me finish,' shot back Gingrich, before launching into another wave of angry rebuke directed full-throttle at his hapless inquisitor. Gingrich, being Gingrich, probably over-played his hand, both in time and in temper. But there was absolutely no doubt as to who came out on top after this verbal firestorm. Gingrich's stock rose dramatically in the polls and 3 days later he walked off with a 12 percentage-point victory in the South Carolina primary, capturing an impressive 40% of the vote.

All eyes were now turned on Florida which was holding its primary 10 days later. So far the first three contests had produced three different winners. Who could now win in this key swing state? It was now that Romney's vastly superior organisation and financial backing paid dividends. Santorum and Paul, realising that Florida was not their kind of state, had barely set foot in the place, and Romney was able to outspend Gingrich four-to-one in a state where television media markets are both expensive and the only realistic way of reaching large numbers of voters. Romney beat Gingrich by 14 percentage points, thereby for the first time establishing himself as the clear frontrunner on the basis of votes cast and delegates won.

It's Santorum again

Five days after his victory in South Carolina, Newt Gingrich was leading the poll-of-polls on the Real Clear Politics website (**www.realclearpolitics.com**) with 31% to Romney's 27% (Table 2.3). Three weeks later, Gingrich's support had collapsed — again — to 14%. On the other hand, Rick Santorum who had been at 4% at the start of January shot up to 16% in the national polls after his win in Iowa was confirmed, but by mid-February was leading the polls at 34% to Romney's 27%. Santorum's second surge was the result of his making a clean sweep of all three contests on 7 February — in Colorado, Minnesota and Missouri (Table 2.2).

Table 2.3 Real Clear Politics poll leaders and second place candidates, 1 August 2011 to 29 February 2012

Dates	Poll leader	Poll second place
1–23 August	Mitt Romney	Michele Bachmann
24 August–3 October	Rick Perry	Mitt Romney
4–19 October	Mitt Romney	Rick Perry and Herman Cain
20 October–10 November	Herman Cain	Mitt Romney
11–20 November	Mitt Romney	Herman Cain and Newt Gingrich
21 November–3 January	Newt Gingrich	Mitt Romney
4–23 January	Mitt Romney	Newt Gingrich
24 January–2 February	Newt Gingrich	Mitt Romney
3–12 February	Mitt Romney	Newt Gingrich and Rick Santorum
13–28 February	Rick Santorum	Mitt Romney
29 February–	Mitt Romney	Rick Santorum

But these victories were somewhat less significant than they appeared. Winning primaries and caucuses is not an end in itself. It's the winning of national convention delegates which is the end in view. The trouble for Santorum was that all these three contests were non-binding, in other words no convention delegates were allocated as a result of them. That would be done later in county, district or state party conventions. And when those three states got around to awarding their convention delegates, Santorum would get just 21 compared with the 77 awarded to Romney.

But there was a short-term benefit for Santorum who returned to the leading position in the poll of polls on 13 February, a position he held for the next fortnight. Meanwhile, the remaining five contests before Super Tuesday — in Maine, Arizona, Michigan, Wyoming and Washington State — were all won by Mitt Romney, with Santorum coming a close second in a number of them. The issue by Super Tuesday therefore was which one of Santorum or Gingrich would survive to carry on the fight against Romney?

Super Tuesday and beyond

Not-so-super Tuesday 6 March was a much smaller and less make-or-break event than it had been in previous election cycles. Ten states were voting, but two were the home states of the three remaining first tier candidates — Romney's Massachusetts and Gingrich's Georgia. The caucuses in Alaska and North Dakota were non-binding preference votes, with delegates being selected later at state party conventions. In Virginia, both Santorum and Gingrich had failed to collect enough signatures to get their names on the ballot paper, thereby giving Romney a free run in a state that would otherwise have been highly competitive. That left only five competitive races for delegates — in Idaho, Ohio, Vermont, Oklahoma and Tennessee — with Romney winning in the first three and Santorum the latter two. But it was his win over Santorum in Ohio — a critical swing state — that was the most important for Governor Romney. True the victory was narrow — by only just over 10,000 votes out of over 1.2 million — but when the delegates were totted up, Romney had won 38 to Santorum's 25.

Through the remainder of March, Santorum picked up wins in Kansas, Alabama, Mississippi and Louisiana, but it was again Romney who won the biggest prize of Illinois, picking up 45 delegates to Santorum's 12. Then on 3 April, Romney had a clean sweep, winning in Maryland, Wisconsin and the District of Columbia. By now the most reliable tally of pledged convention delegates gave Romney 658 to Santorum's 281 and just 135 for Gingrich. It was now well nigh impossible for Santorum to overhaul Romney's substantial lead in delegates with only 19 contests remaining. On 10 April, Santorum bowed to the inevitable and suspended his campaign. This was also the day on which the website Real Clear Politics first recorded Romney with a 40% rating in its poll of polls. Gingrich — now the only viable alternative to Romney — had meanwhile slumped to fourth place on 11%, even below Ron Paul.

Romney notched up another five straight victories on 24 April, including New York and Pennsylvania, with Gingrich struggling to even get over 10% in most of them. Even Newt Gingrich was not pig-headed enough to carry on in the light of such a thrashing and on 2 May the former House Speaker also bowed out. That left the enigmatic congressman from Texas, Ron Paul, who batted on for a further 2 weeks before he too called it a day. Paul's unique brand of conservatism and libertarianism appeals to those who share his minimalist view of the role of government — especially the federal government. It is Paul's appeal to the out-of-the-mainstream voter that boosts his support in those states which hold caucuses, where the turnout is higher among the more ideological voters. His average vote in the 12 caucus states was just over 21% whereas his average share of the vote across all the contests — primaries and caucuses — was nearer 10%.

The party's national convention in Tampa, Florida, in late August would be attended by 2,286 delegates. Romney's win in the Texas primary on 29 May put him over the 1,144 delegates (50% plus one) required to win the nomination. As Table 2.4 shows, this was significantly later in the year than the previously contested

Table 2.4 Date upon which Republican presidential nomination secured, 1988–2012 (contested nominations only)

Year	Republican nominee	Date nomination secured
1988	George H. W. Bush	26 April
1996	Bob Dole	26 March
2000	George W. Bush	16 March
2008	John McCain	5 February
2012	Mitt Romney	29 May

Republican nominations had been secured and almost 4 months later than John McCain had secured the party's nomination in 2008. But this was largely due to the changes in the calendar and the party rules, especially the resulting decline in winner-takes-all primaries.

Briefly about Obama

Like presidents Bill Clinton (1996) and George W. Bush (2004), Barack Obama did not receive any serious challenge for his re-nomination. Although there were the usual Democratic primaries and caucuses running from January to June of 2012, they consequently received little or no coverage. In most states, the President was the only candidate on the ballot and in 10 states he received 100% of the votes as well as all the delegates. But what was somewhat surprising was that the President failed to reach 90% in 14 states and in four states he failed to reach 60%, meaning that lightweight opponents or voters voting 'uncommitted' received more than 40% (Table 2.5).

Incumbent presidents have been known to lose votes in primaries to well-known national figures. President Ford lost votes to Ronald Reagan in the 1976 Republican primaries, President Carter to Senator Ted Kennedy in the 1980 Democratic primaries and President George H. W. Bush to Pat Buchanan in the 1992 Republican primaries. But the folk who were gaining up to 40% of the vote

Table 2.5 Democratic presidential primary results, 2012 (selected states)

State	Candidates	Percentage
Oklahoma	**Barack Obama**	**57.1**
	Terry Randall	18.0
	Jim Rogers	13.8
	Darcy Richardson	6.4
	Bob Moulton-Ely	4.7
Kentucky	**Barack Obama**	**57.9**
	Uncommitted	42.1
Arkansas	**Barack Obama**	**58.3**
	John Wolfe	41.7
West Virginia	**Barack Obama**	**59.3**
	Keith Judd	40.7
Louisiana	**Barack Obama**	**76.5**
	John Wolfe	11.8
	Bob Moulton-Ely	6.6
	Darcy Richardson	5.2
Texas	**Barack Obama**	**76.7**
	Darcy Richardson	15.8
	John Wolfe	5.1
	Bob Moulton-Ely	2.5

Table 2.6 Percentage of primary vote won by incumbent presidents, 1976–2012

President	Party	Year	Percentage of primary vote	Election result
Ronald Reagan	R	1984	99	Won
George W. Bush	R	2004	98	Won
Barack Obama	**Dem**	**2012**	**92**	**Won**
Bill Clinton	Dem	1996	89	Won
George H. W. Bush	R	1992	72	Lost
Gerald Ford	R	1976	53	Lost
Jimmy Carter	Dem	1980	51	Lost

Source: The Rhodes Cook Letter, June 2012

in these states against President Obama in 2012 were not candidates of that ilk. In Arkansas, the President lost over 41% of the vote to John Wolfe. Mr Wolfe ran for the mayoralty of Chattanooga in his home state of Tennessee in 1998 and got less than 3% of the vote and has lost four races for Congress. Yet here he was winning 41% of the vote against the President in Arkansas, nearly 12% in Louisiana and over 5% in Texas.

Even more extraordinary was the 40% garnered by Keith Judd in the West Virginia Democratic primary. At the time, Mr Judd was otherwise known as Inmate Number 11593-051 in a Texas state prison where he had been since 1999, serving a lengthy prison sentence for extortion.

None of this really seemed to matter at the time, and the President was never in danger of failing to be re-nominated, but here were some early telltale signs that in some states at least, President Obama was not hugely popular, even among likely Democratic voters and even when the opposition was somewhat dubious. Even Governor Romney might pose a greater threat to the President than John Wolfe and Keith Judd. And as Table 2.6 shows, President Obama's overall primary performance compared favourably with that of recent incumbent presidents.

Turnout

Another way to measure enthusiasm levels in the two major parties is to look at turnout levels in the primaries and compare them with previous nomination cycles. Table 2.7 compares the Republican turnout in ten states between 2008 and 2012. The first five were all states that scheduled their primaries early in both nomination cycles and voted in both cycles before the nomination had been decided. All five states saw an increase in voting levels on 4 years ago, with increases of between 4 and 36 percentage points.

Both California and New York scheduled their primaries much later in 2012 than they had done in 2008. Therefore whereas in 2008 the nomination was still open when they voted, in 2012 Romney had already virtually sewn up the contest.

Table 2.7 Turnout in selected Republican primaries: 2008 and 2012 compared

State	2008 turnout	2012 turnout	% change
New Hampshire	238,328	248,475	+4
Michigan	868,083	996,126	+15
South Carolina	443,203	603,770	+36
Arizona	451,584	508,160	+13
Ohio	1,062,276	1,203,403	+13
California	2,251,236	1,924,970	−14
New York	605,529	190,515	−69
Mississippi	143,286	294,112	+105
Indiana	411,948	623,771	+51
North Carolina	522,635	973,206	+86

Hence both states saw a fall in primary turnout. This was much steeper in New York than in California as the latter state, although moving its presidential primary from February to June, coincided it in 2012 with the state's congressional primaries, thereby encouraging quite a high turnout. New York, on the other hand, merely moved its presidential primary from early February to late April and did not coincide it with any other state elections, hence the precipitate fall in turnout.

Mississippi, Indiana and North Carolina held their primaries late in the cycle in both 2008 and 2012. But whereas by the time these states voted in 2008 John McCain had already secured the nomination, in 2012 these states voted before Romney had secured the necessary number of delegates and hence the significant increase in turnout. Overall, turnout in the Republican primaries was relatively healthy, down only slightly from 20.8 million in 2008 to 18.7 million in 2012 (Figure 2.1). Of the 38 states that held Republican primaries in both 2008 and 2012, turnout increased in 16 states and decreased in 22.

Obviously one cannot compare primary turnout in the 2012 Democratic primaries with turnout in 2008. In 2008, there was an exciting and close contest fought between Barack Obama and Hillary Clinton, whereas this time around President Obama was the only serious candidate. One would therefore need to go back to 1996 — the year when another Democratic president, Bill Clinton, was unopposed in the primaries. In that year, nearly 11 million voters took part in the Democratic primaries. But in 2012 only 9 million took part — a significant fall in voter commitment and enthusiasm. Indeed, this was the smallest turnout in any Democratic presidential primary cycle since the 1960s. Thus although the White House seemed relatively sanguine about facing Mitt Romney in the fall campaign, there were already some worrying signs for the President — electorally as well as economically.

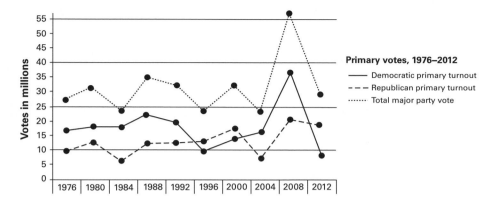

Primary votes, 1976–2012

—— Democratic primary turnout

– – – Republican primary turnout

········· Total major party vote

Figure 2.1 Voter turnout in presidential primaries, 1976–2012

Source: The Rhodes Cook Letter, June 2012

Questions

1 What changes did the Republican National Committee make in its rules for selecting presidential candidates and convention delegates in 2012?
2 To what extent did state Republican parties keep to these new rules?
3 What were the effects of these rule changes?
4 What did we learn in 2012 about the importance, or otherwise, of Iowa in the selection of presidential candidates?
5 From which voters did Rick Santorum gain his strongest support?
6 How did Newt Gingrich use the television debate just before the South Carolina primary to boost his chances of winning the primary?
7 Why were Santorum's three wins on 7 February not that significant?
8 Explain why Super Tuesday in 2012 was less important than it had been in 2008.
9 Explain the significance of the data presented in Table 2.4.
10 What concerns for President Obama did the Democratic primaries of 2012 show up?
11 How did voter turnout in the Republican and Democratic primaries compare with previous nomination cycles?

Chapter 3

From the primaries to the conventions

What you need to know

- The primaries and caucuses finish in June.
- The national party conventions are not held until late August or early September.
- Traditionally, the presidential nominee of the challenging party did not announce his vice-presidential candidate until the convention, but nowadays this announcement is made in the period between the primaries and the conventions.
- The vice-presidential candidate — otherwise known as the running-mate — is chosen solely by the presidential candidate.
- These two candidates then run as a joint 'ticket' in the general election campaign and are elected — or defeated — together in November.

The Obama and Romney campaigns begin

As August 2012 broke and most of the USA sweltered in alarmingly hot temperatures, the climate of the presidential race remained somewhat tepid. President Obama was to be re-nominated by the Democratic Party without any serious challenge and Governor Romney's challengers in the Republican Party had by now mostly faded into oblivion. For the past 2 months, little of note had happened. True, Mitt Romney had made a tour of some European capitals which had raised a few eyebrows with some noted foot-in-mouth comments. 'MITT THE TWIT' screamed the headline in Britain's *Sun* newspaper after Romney had managed to annoy both the prime minister, David Cameron, and opposition leader, Ed Miliband, within a 24-hour period.

President Obama was not bothering with foreign travel, preferring to spend his time touring the USA for fundraisers and other campaign-related events. In the 4-week period immediately following the Fourth of July holiday, the President travelled over 20,000 miles, visiting 11 states including three trips to both Ohio and Virginia, and two to Florida (Table 3.1) — all key swing states in the upcoming campaign. Excluding weekends, there were only 4 days when the President did not leave Washington DC for a campaign or fundraising event. On 9 days he travelled in excess of 1,000 miles in a day.

Table 3.1 President Obama's campaign schedule, 5 July–2 August

Date	Travelled to	Miles travelled
5 July	Toledo, Ohio	471
6 July	Pittsburgh, Pennsylvania	233
9 July	Washington DC	246
10 July	Cedar Rapids, Iowa [Returns to Washington DC]	1,860
13 July	Norfolk, Virginia Hampton, Virginia Roanoke, Virginia [Returns to Washington DC]	450
16 July	Cincinnati, Ohio	1,004
17 July	San Antonio, Texas	1,602
	Austin, Texas	80
18 July	Washington DC	1,525
19 July	Jacksonville, Florida	345
	West Palm Beach, Florida	285
20 July	Fort Myers, Florida	125
	[Returns to Washington DC]	1,020
22 July	San Francisco, California	2,814
23 July	Reno, Nevada	218
	Oakland, California	212
24 July	Portland, Oregon	630
	Seattle, Washington	175
25 July	New Orleans, Louisiana	2,712
27 July	Washington DC	1,084
	McLean, Virginia	20
30 July	New York City, New York [Returns to Washington DC]	454
1 Aug	Mansfield, Ohio	408
	Akron, Ohio	65
	[Returns to Washington DC]	351
2 Aug	Orlando, Florida	851
	Leesburg, Virginia	870
	[Returns to Washington DC]	41
TOTAL		20,151

Source: www.whitehouse.gov/schedule/president

Table 3.2 Fundraising of Big Four super PACs to 11 August, 2012

Super PAC	Viewpoint	Supports	Total raised ($)
Restore Our Future	Conservative	Mitt Romney	82,200,973
American Crossroads	Conservative	–	40,233,419
Winning Our Future	Conservative	Newt Gingrich	23,921,115
Priorities USA Action	Liberal	Barack Obama	20,736,737

A new fundraising environment

The President was also benefiting from incumbency in terms of fundraising. By the beginning of August, Obama had raised just over $300 million to Romney's $154 million. But following the *Citizens United* v *Federal Election Commission* decision by the Supreme Court in 2010 this presidential election cycle would not just be about what the candidates' organisations and the major parties would raise and spend, but also about what the new 'super PACs' would be raising and spending. The 2010 decision allowed both corporate groups and labour unions to spend as much as they wanted on behalf of the candidates they wished to support provided they spent it independently. This led to the formation of what have become known as 'super PACs'. (PAC is an abbreviation for Political Action Committee.) These new super PACs can receive unlimited corporate, union and individual contributions and then spend that money to advocate the election or defeat of any candidate for federal office, including presidential candidates.

By 11 August, just over 2 weeks before the opening of the Republican National Convention, super PACs had already raised between them in excess of $300 million. Almost half of that amount had been raised by just four super-super PACs (Table 3.2) of which three had been established to work for the election of 'conservative' (i.e. Republican) candidates. The largest by far in terms of money raised was Restore Our Future which had raised over $82 million by this time and was committed to the election of Mitt Romney to the White House. A visit to its website made this very clear as Box 3.1 shows. Another conservative super PAC,

Box 3.1   Restore Our Future

Widespread unemployment. Businesses tied in red tape and shackled by the federal government. Our nation's bottom line threatened by excessive spending and seemingly endless government. America is at a historic crossroads, yet President Obama has failed to devise real solutions or prompt meaningful actions to address the problems facing workers, job creators, and the American financial system.

There is only one candidate who has the experience to stop the reckless spending, and bring down our national debt. That candidate is Mitt Romney.

Help Mitt Romney become our next President. Donate today.

Source: www.restoreourfuture.com/about

American Crossroads, had thus far spent around $11.7 million of which almost $9 million had been spent campaigning against President Obama.

Romney chooses Ryan

'The bottom line about virtually all vice-presidential picks is that they seem far more important to the campaign when they're made than they turn out to be,' commented Jonathan Bernstein on the *Washington Post* website within minutes of Mitt Romney's selection of Congressman Paul Ryan as his running-mate.

There were four remarkable facts about the selection of Congressman Paul Ryan of Wisconsin as the Republican vice-presidential nominee. The first concerned the timing. Romney made the announcement aboard the *USS Wisconsin* in Norfolk, Virginia, on the morning of Saturday 11 August — 16 days before the scheduled opening of the Republican National Party Convention. It used to be the case that vice-presidential candidates were chosen by the convention. When the choosing passed to the presidential candidate himself, the announcement was still made during the convention — that is until 1984. That year, the Democrat presidential candidate Walter Mondale announced his running-mate — Congresswoman Geraldine Ferraro of New York — 4 days before the convention. All subsequent Democratic Party vice-presidential nominees were announced ahead of the convention — 20 days before in 2004. But the Republicans took until 1996 to follow suit when Bob Dole announced his choice of Jack Kemp 1 day before the party's convention. The selections of Dick Cheney (2000) and Sarah Palin (2008) were also announced a few days ahead of the convention. But never before had a Republican running-mate been announced over 2 weeks ahead of the convention. This fact itself showed how keen Romney was to try to shake up the race.

Second, the running-mate's political background was something of a surprise — that he was a serving member of the House of Representatives. Of all the Republican vice-presidential (VP) candidates going back to William Dayton in 1856, ten have been senators and seven state governors. But only once in the last 100 years had the Republican vice-presidential candidate been an incumbent member of the House and that was William Miller of New York in 1964.

Third, the vice-presidential candidate's age was remarkable. At 42, Ryan was the youngest running-mate of either major party since Senator Dan Quayle had been chosen in 1988 at the age of 41. Indeed, the average age of the 11 vice-presidential candidates chosen between 1980 and 2008 had been 54. So Ryan at 42 was clearly an unusual pick (Table 3.3). Going further back in political history, Ryan was tied as the sixth youngest vice-presidential nominee on a major party ticket (Table 3.4).

The fourth unusual fact about Paul Ryan's selection as Romney's running-mate was that he comes from Wisconsin, a state which had never before had one of its native sons nominated as a vice-presidential candidate. If one traces the list back to 1824 and includes all vice-presidential candidates of any party which won at least one Electoral College vote then Ryan was the 91st such candidate but

Table 3.3 Vice-presidential (VP) candidates by age, 1980–2012

VP candidate	Party	Year	Age
Dan Quayle	R	1988	41
Paul Ryan	**R**	**2012**	**42**
Al Gore	Dem	1992	44
Sarah Palin	R	2008	44
Geraldine Ferraro	Dem	1984	48
John Edwards	Dem	2004	51
George H. W. Bush	R	1980	56
Joe Lieberman	Dem	2000	58
Dick Cheney	R	2000	59
Jack Kemp	R	1996	61
Joe Biden	Dem	2008	65
Lloyd Bentsen	Dem	1988	67

Table 3.4 Youngest major party vice-presidential candidates

VP candidate	Party	Year	Age
John Breckenridge	Dem	1856	35
Franklin D. Roosevelt	Dem	1920	38
Richard Nixon	R	1952	39
George Pendleton	Dem	1864	39
Dan Quayle	R	1988	41
Paul Ryan	**R**	**2012**	**42**
Theodore Roosevelt	R	1900	42
John Calhoun	D-R	1824	42
Daniel Tompkins	D-R	1816	42
Francis Granger	Whig	1836	43
Sarah Palin	R	2008	44
Al Gore	Dem	1992	44
Aaron Burr	D-R	1800	44

Table 3.5 Selected major party tickets, 1976–2012

Year	Presidential candidate	Political experience	VP candidate	Political experience
1976	Jimmy Carter	Governor	Walter Mondale	Congress
1980	Ronald Reagan	Governor	George H. W. Bush	Congress/ Executive
1988	Michael Dukakis	Governor	Lloyd Bentsen	Congress
1992	Bill Clinton	Governor	Al Gore	Congress
2000	George W. Bush	Governor	Dick Cheney	Congress/ Executive
2012	**Mitt Romney**	**Governor**	**Paul Ryan**	**Congress**

the first from Wisconsin. In contrast, New York has provided 15 vice-presidential nominees during that period, including Jack Kemp in 1996 and Geraldine Ferraro in 1984.

But in another respect, Romney's selection of Ryan fitted a familiar pattern of a presidential candidate who either was or had been a state governor selecting a member of Congress as his running-mate. Jimmy Carter, Ronald Reagan, Michael Dukakis and George W. Bush had all trodden this road as is shown in Table 3.5.

The Ryan selection was familiar in another sense in that Romney had chosen a political insider — someone who had grafted his way up the party political ladder — rather than an outsider (Table 3.6). The 'insiders' are folk who had previously served in senior political positions — as national party chairman (Bush), long-time member of Congress (Bentsen and Biden), cabinet member (Kemp), White House chief of staff (Cheney), or congressional committee chairman (Ryan). Some of them had even run — unsuccessfully — as a presidential candidate, namely Bush, Gore, Kemp and Biden. The 'outsiders' were political unknowns at the time of their selection with little political experience or seniority. In contrast to Ryan's seven terms in the House of Representatives and his status as chairman of the House Budget Committee, Geraldine Ferraro had served only three terms in the House and held no position of leadership or seniority when she was selected in 1984. Sarah Palin had served less than 2 years as governor of Alaska when she was picked as John McCain's running-mate in 2008.

Table 3.6 Insider/outsider status of vice-presidential candidates, 1980–2012

Year	VP candidate	Party	Insider/outsider
1980	George H. W. Bush	R	Insider
1984	Geraldine Ferraro	Dem	Outsider
1988	Dan Quayle	R	Outsider
	Lloyd Bentsen	Dem	Insider
1992	Al Gore	Dem	Insider
1996	Jack Kemp	R	Insider
2000	Dick Cheney	R	Insider
	Joe Lieberman	Dem	Insider
2004	John Edwards	Dem	Outsider
2008	Joe Biden	Dem	Insider
	Sarah Palin	R	Outsider
2012	**Paul Ryan**	**R**	**Insider**

But for all the media hype and excitement, VP picks are much overrated. As Ari Fleischer, a former Bush administration official, commented in the *Washington Post* 2 days before the Ryan pick: 'VP picks can provide a temporary burst of excitement to a ticket, but pretty soon things settle down and the race is once again about the man at the top.' This year, even the 'temporary burst of excitement'

seemed to be missing. On the day on which Romney made his announcement, the Gallup daily tracking poll had the race tied at 46%–46%. Two days later, Romney's poll number ticked up to 47% and Obama's down to 45%. Ten days later, the numbers were back to 46–46. That was the extent of the Ryan burst of excitement. That left only the Republican convention and the television debates for Romney to change the numbers in his favour.

Questions

1 Analyse the data presented in Table 3.1.
2 What are super PACS? How did they come about? Give two examples.
3 In what four ways was Romney's selection of Paul Ryan as his running-mate unusual?
4 Give two ways in which the selection of Ryan followed previous selection patterns.
5 What immediate effect did the selection of Ryan have on Romney's poll numbers?

Chapter 4

The conventions: more than banners and balloons?

What you need to know

- National party conventions meet for about 4 days during the late summer of the presidential election year.
- By tradition, the 'challenging party' — the Republicans in 2012 — holds its convention first.
- The conventions are attended by the delegates who are mostly chosen during the primaries and caucuses.
- The conventions are said to have three main functions: choosing the party's presidential candidate; choosing the party's vice-presidential candidate; deciding on the party platform, i.e. the manifesto.
- But nowadays all three functions are done before the conventions meet.
- The significance of modern-day conventions is therefore questionable.

The Republicans in Tampa

The Republicans gathered for their convention on Monday 27 August in Tampa, Florida, but due to the effects of Tropical Storm Isaac, the party decided to postpone the start of formal business until the following day. Present at the convention were the 2,286 delegates chosen mostly in the primaries and caucuses held between January and June. The largest delegation was the 172 delegates from California; the smallest state delegation was the 12 from New Hampshire. That fact alone makes one wonder again about the excitement surrounding the New Hampshire primary.

On the Tuesday, the delegates ratified the party platform under its bland title of 'We believe in America'. There's always the danger that we think of a party platform as the US equivalent of the party manifesto in the UK. But whereas the latter is regarded as something of a contract between the party and the voters, the former is of nowhere near the same importance. In the UK, party manifestos contain 'promises' and a party elected to government is then expected to fulfil these promises before the next election or face the anger of the voters. Woe betide a party that breaks its manifesto promises once in government — think tuition fees. Times used to be when there would be fierce debates at the respective US party conventions on controversial issues in the platform — think Democrats over the Vietnam War in 1968 or Republicans over women's rights in 1980 or abortion in 1992. But these days, the major US parties tend to shy away from 'floor fights'. The public watching on television see them as signs of internal division and squabbling and tend to react negatively.

The US party platforms tend to be a collection of somewhat bland generalities and universally accepted clichés and favourite words. Take the 2012 Republican platform in which the word 'opportunity' occurred 21 times, including six times on the opening page. There were references to 'the pursuit of opportunity', 'the land of opportunity', 'a dream of equal opportunity', 'an opportunity society' and 'economic opportunity' — indeed, the Republican Party is, so we are told, 'the opportunity party', even the 'Grand Opportunity Party'.

That said, there was plenty in the 2012 Republican Party platform that clearly distinguished it from the document put out by the Democrats. The Republican platform supported:

- a constitutional amendment defining marriage as the union of one man and one woman
- a Balanced Budget Amendment to the Constitution
- the public display of the Ten Commandments
- the right of students to engage in prayer in public [i.e. state-run] schools
- the right of individuals to keep and bear arms
- the sanctity of human life including that of the unborn child
- legal protection against desecration for the American flag
- the expansion of nuclear energy
- reining in the power of the Environmental Protection Agency
- repeal of the Patient Protection and Affordable Care Act ('Obamacare')
- consumer choice in education
- unequivocal support for Israel

There is no possibility of mistaking that as a list of the *Democratic* Party's policy preferences. Supporting these policies is what distinguishes a true Republican from a Democrat. But the list raises the question of how many — if any — of these policies could be pursued by a future Romney administration. Many would require action by Congress — certainly not a given these days, even if the president's party were to enjoy majorities in both houses. Others — such as those calling for a constitutional amendment — would require super-majorities in Congress and the agreement of at least three-quarters of the state legislatures, while others would require the compliance of the judiciary who are not known to be under the control of the president — no matter which party.

The traditional roll-call of the states occurred on the Tuesday — the first full day of the convention. Most of Romney's opponents from the primaries — Rick Santorum, Newt Gingrich and company — had by now formally endorsed Romney as their preferred candidate and released their delegates to cast a vote for Romney. This is usual practice and helps promote much-needed party unity. The only candidate who had not done this was Ron Paul, hoping by holding on to his delegates to gain influence in the platform debates. But when the vote came it was well nigh unanimous with 2,061 of the 2,286 delegates voting for Romney, just 190 for Ron Paul and some scattered votes for other former candidates. Paul Ryan was confirmed as vice-presidential candidate by a voice vote. Big-name Tuesday evening speakers included Rick Santorum, the governor of New Jersey Chris Christie, as well as Ann Romney. Conventions can be used to showcase possible future presidential nominees and both Santorum and Christie would fall into that category.

Paul Ryan's acceptance speech on the Wednesday fell foul of many political commentators and so-called fact checkers. The same day saw the appearance of some Republican big names from past eras, including 2008 presidential nominee John McCain and former secretary of state Condoleezza Rice, though notably absent were both George H. W. and George W. Bush.

There were two talking points from the final evening when really there should only have been one — Mitt Romney's acceptance speech. But before they got to that, the audience — both in the hall and at home on television — had to endure an excruciatingly embarrassing performance by the ageing film star Clint Eastwood. Equipped with an empty chair as a prop and with the Romney team having no idea what he was going to say, Eastwood meandered through a routine which was presumably meant to be comic but merely wandered aimlessly between 'cringing' and 'crude'. It was clearly a gross error of judgement on the part of the Romney folk to give such a primetime slot to an unscripted loose cannon.

Republican conventions have not exactly been spoilt by a string of great orators in recent years — think Bob Dole or George W. Bush. But by most impartial assessments, the Romney speech failed even to meet its low expectations, leaving many longing for a Dole witticism or a much-loved Bush-ism. The Romney speech was dull, wooden and almost entirely unmemorable. Hardly surprising, when one discovered the chaotic and last-minute process by which it had been written, that it sounded like the cobbled-together jumble of paragraphs which it truly was. There was not even a mention of or a tribute to US armed forces serving oversees or those who had died in the service of their country. 'You may not always agree with me, but you know where I stand,' was a memorable and important line from Bush's 2004 acceptance speech. When one is left idolising a George W. Bush speech, one instinctively knows that something is wrong.

Party conventions are not an end in themselves — they are a means to an end. And the ultimate aim is to gather new found momentum for your nominee. It's what we call 'bounce' — the increase in the poll rating for the presidential nominee as a result of the party convention (Table 4.1). The average bounce for a candidate coming out of his convention in the last four election cycles — from 1996 through 2008 — was just over 4 percentage points. Romney got no bounce at all. Indeed, according to the Gallup poll — probably the most reliable — Romney suffered a dip of 1 percentage point. The only other candidate to receive a negative bounce since the 1960s was John Kerry, the Democratic candidate in 2004. It was the worst post-convention bounce for a Republican since polling began in 1964. Romney, behind in the polls, had seemingly blown another opportunity to shake up this race to his advantage: the primaries hadn't done it; his selection of Paul Ryan hadn't done it; now the Republican convention hadn't done it either. Time was running out for Romney as all eyes shifted from Tampa to Charlotte.

Table 4.1 Post-convention 'bounce', 1996–2012

Year	Challenging party candidate	Bounce	Incumbent party candidate	Bounce
1996	Bob Dole (R)	+3	Bill Clinton (D)	+5
2000	George W. Bush (R)	+8	Al Gore (D)	+8
2004	John Kerry (D)	–1	George W. Bush (R)	+2
2008	Barack Obama (D)	+4	John McCain (R)	+6
2012	Mitt Romney (R)	–1	Barack Obama (D)	+3

The Democrats in Charlotte, North Carolina

The Democrats gathered in Charlotte for their convention the week after the Republicans had concluded theirs in Tampa. While the Republicans had scheduled 4 days for their convention, the Democrats had cut theirs to 3 days. Obama's Democrats had reasons both for optimism and concern. On the upside, they were a united party with Obama having been acclaimed their party's presidential nominee without any significant opposition. That was what had happened to Nixon in 1972, Reagan in 1984, Clinton in 1996 and Bush in 2004, and all those presidents had gone on to win re-election. They had confidence too in the campaigning and debating skills of both Obama and Vice President Biden. And the campaign was certainly not short of money, especially having not had the expense of an intra-party contest during the first half of the year.

But on the downside, there was much statistical evidence — on the economy, on the President's approval rating, and on voters' views of the direction the country was heading — that gave significant cause for concern. After all, a president presiding over unemployment at 8%, with approval ratings stuck under 50% and with the vast majority of Americans believing the country was 'on the wrong track' was hardly a sure bet for re-election. It was these and similar circumstances that had sunk Presidents Ford (1976), Carter (1980) and Bush (1992). So the convention was an important opportunity for the President to rally the troops and convince the voters to 'stay the course'.

The star of the first day was the primetime speech by First Lady Michelle Obama who spoke eloquently of the President, reminding her audience that 'change takes time'. The highlight of the second day was the much-anticipated speech by former president Bill Clinton. Inviting Clinton to take the spotlight was a bold move by the President. He and Clinton haven't always had the smoothest of relationships and Clinton has a track record of delivering speeches littered with the first person singular pronoun. Obama need not have worried. This was a barnstormer of a speech and, pitched at independent and swing voters, as well as disenchanted Democrats, it was pitch perfect. He went through the Republicans' policies one-by-one and offered a simple critique of each. He went through their accusations against the President and begged for voters' patience to stay the course with Barack Obama. It was vibrant, detailed, inspiring, amusing — it was Clinton at his best. The only downside of the speech was that it was widely reviewed as being better than the President's acceptance speech which came on the final night.

This was when the Democrats had their brush with the weather too. The last night should have been staged outdoors at the 72,000-seater Bank of America Stadium but the threat of bad weather forced the Democrats into the 20,000-seat indoor arena instead. Or did it? Some in the media suggested that the move had more to do with the fear of empty seats than of wet delegates. In his acceptance speech, Obama, like Clinton the previous evening, tried to convince the doubters, the impatient, those who had lost faith in the much-promised 'change we can believe in', of his 2008 slogan. Now, 4 years later, the President stated: 'I never said this journey would be easy, and I won't promise that now.' He admitted that 'yes, our road is longer' than he had thought. But, he warned, 'if you turn away now, if you buy into the cynicism that the change we fought for isn't possible, then change will not happen'. As Table 4.1 shows, Obama came away from the convention with a 3 percentage-point bounce, and for a candidate already in the lead, that was good enough. But put in historical context, it was the weakest post-convention bounce for an incumbent Democratic nominee since Lyndon Johnson's three-point bounce in 1964.

What use are conventions?

According to a Gallup poll published on 10 September, both conventions did little to advance the cause of either party or their nominee. As the data presented in Table 4.2 show, the net impact of both conventions was the weakest for each party in over 30 years, with the Democrat convention having a net impact on voting intentions of plus 5 and the Republican convention a mere plus 2.

When it came to rating the acceptance speeches of the two presidential candidates, both Romney's and Obama's received less than ecstatic praise. Those rating Romney's speech as 'excellent' or 'good' totalled just 38% — lower than McCain in 2008 (47%), Bush in 2004 (49%), Bush in 2000 (51%) and even Dole in 1996 (52%). Those rating Obama's speech in these two categories totalled 43% — well below Gore in 2000 (51%), Kerry in 2004 (52%) and his own speech in 2008 (58%). Sixteen percent of respondents rated the speeches as 'terrible'. Twelve years ago, only 6% rated Al Gore's speech as 'terrible' and just 4% George W. Bush's. There was some evidence that President Obama had been overshadowed by former president Bill Clinton's speech. While only 43% rated Obama's speech as 'excellent' or 'good', Bill Clinton's speech was so described by 56% of respondents.

Both conventions also failed to attract television viewers in the numbers which were achieved in 2008 (Table 4.3). The percentage of those saying they watched 'a great deal' or 'some' of the Democratic convention fell from 60% in 2008 to 55% in 2012, while those watching similar amounts of the Republican convention fell dramatically from 71% to 51%.

Table 4.2 Does what you saw/read of this week's Republican/Democratic convention make you more/less likely to vote for the Republican/Democratic candidate for president?

Convention	More likely	Less likely	No difference	Net impact
1992 Democrat (Clinton)	60	15	25	45
1988 Democrat (Dukakis)	56	21	23	35
2000 Republican (Bush)	44	27	29	17
1988 Republican (Bush)	43	27	30	16
1984 Democrat (Mondale)	45	29	26	16
1996 Democrat (Clinton)	44	29	27	15
2000 Democrat (Gore)	43	28	29	15
2004 Democrat (Kerry)	44	30	26	14
2008 Democrat (Obama)	43	29	27	14
1996 Republican (Dole)	45	34	21	11
2008 Republican (McCain)	43	38	19	5
2012 Democrat (Obama)	**43**	**38**	**20**	**5**
2004 Republican (Bush)	41	38	21	3
2012 Republican (Romney)	**40**	**38**	**21**	**2**

Source: **www.gallup.com**

Table 4.3 How much if any of the Republican/Democratic convention did you watch on television this week?

Convention	Watched a great deal/ some (%)
Republican 2008	71
Republican 2004	63
Democratic 2008	60
Democratic 2004	59
Republican 2000	56
Democratic 2012	**55**
Democratic 2000	55
Republican 2012	**51**
Republican 1996	45

Source: **www.gallup.com**

Once both conventions were wrapped up, an editorial in the *Los Angeles Times* (9 September, 2012) had this to say:

> Like the Republican convention that preceded it, the Democratic National Convention was a combination of infomercial, revival meeting (with former President Clinton in the role of Evangelist in Chief) and audition for rising political stars.

Time was when the party convention was the great highlight of election year — a quadrennial event which received extensive coverage on the terrestrial television channels, which is all there were in those days. They made decisions; they chose candidates; they made policy decisions. They were real political theatre. But over the decades, conventions have fallen victim to direct primaries where the presidential candidate is now chosen, ever-earlier announcements regarding the identity of the VP candidate, and the plethora of television channels which give viewers the option to switch away from the party conventions. That's not to say that modern day conventions are completely pointless — witness the quotation above. But will they still be around in two decades' time? Maybe not.

In 2012, both parties reduced their conventions from 4- to 3-day events — the Republicans by accident because of weather-related events, the Democrats by design. Maybe future conventions will be even shorter. Conventions are expensive to stage, running into hundreds of millions of dollars. The party hierarchy will have to start asking whether such money is well spent. Given the small shifts we've seen in public opinion as a result of them in recent years (Table 4.1) and their declining television appeal, it might not be surprising if someone pulls the plug on them before too long.

Questions

1 In what ways do party platforms in the USA differ from party manifestos in the UK?
2 Give three important policy items listed in the Republican Party platform in 2012.
3 What criticisms were made of Romney's acceptance speech?
4 What concerns were there for Romney after the convention?
5 What were the upside and downside of President Obama's position at this stage in the campaign?
6 Why was Bill Clinton's speech at the Democratic convention so effective?
7 What arguments were made at the Democratic convention for re-electing the President?
8 Analyse the data presented in Tables 4.2 and 4.3.

Chapter 5

The campaign: 'change' or 'more of the same'?

Presidential election campaigns which feature an incumbent president running for re-election — 1996, 2004 and 2012 — are usually part referendum on the past 4 years and part a decision about the future — the next 4 years. Some presidents running for re-election — Reagan in 1984, Bush in 2004 — like the idea of a referendum. There were significant successes to which they could point during their first term which might lead voters to conclude they would do well to vote for 'four more years'. But some presidents — Clinton in 1996 and Obama in 2012 — would need to focus more on the future given that the general assessment of their first 4 years was less than enthusiastic. In 1996, Bill Clinton certainly did not want a referendum on his first 4 years so he successfully focused the election on the future — a promise to build 'a bridge to the twenty-first century'. In 2012, most impartial commentators, including this one, believed that Obama would probably lose an election which focused on the past 4 years. The President therefore would do well to focus on why voters should want a second Obama term.

The strength of the opposition

I still remember suggesting to some American friends of mine back in 1996 that President Clinton might well lose his re-election bid that year. 'Yes,' came back the reply, 'but you can't beat somebody with nobody.' Maybe 'nobody' was a rather harsh judgement of Senator Bob Dole, Clinton's opponent that November. But Dole, for all his likable traits — and, yes, he does have some — was not a strong opponent and Clinton had little difficulty dispatching the Dole campaign and securing a second term by a comfortable margin. So the strength — or weakness — of the opposition is also a very important ingredient in such elections. Presidents Ronald Reagan (1984) and George W. Bush (2004) were blessed with somewhat weak and ineffective opponents in, respectively, Walter Mondale and John Kerry. On the other hand President Jimmy Carter (1980) had the misfortune to be pitted against 'the Great Communicator' — Ronald Reagan.

By the time the general election campaign got underway in earnest in early September 2012, Mitt Romney looked more like a Mondale than a Reagan. It was said of Mondale in 1984 that 'as long as [voters] believed that he lacked presidential qualities, particularly strong leadership, it would block their response to his overtures'. It was also said of Mondale that he was 'well-respected but not well-liked'. Likeability is important in a presidential campaign. Like Mondale and Kerry, Romney had also proved something of a gaffe machine. We have quoted examples in earlier chapters but he was still at it. Campaigning in Michigan, Romney made an unfortunate reference to the clearly false accusations against the President that he is not a 'natural born American citizen' and therefore ought not to be president. 'No one's ever asked to see my birth certificate,' stated Romney. 'They know that this is the place I was born and raised.'

Then on 11 September, a deadly attack was made by heavily armed terrorists on the US Consulate in Benghazi, Libya, killing the US ambassador to Libya, Christopher Stevens. Initially, the Obama administration tried to suggest that this attack was linked to the publicity surrounding an anti-Islamic film made in the USA released via the internet, but this was later proved to be wrong. The attack was pre-planned and carried out by a trained squad, not a spontaneous attack by protesters. However, just before the attack at Benghazi occurred, the US Embassy in Cairo had issued a statement condemning 'the continuing efforts by misguided individuals to hurt the religious feelings of Muslims'. As news of the Benghazi attack began to filter through, Mitt Romney, though not in possession of the facts, decided to use the incident as an occasion to attack the President and his administration.

> I'm outraged by the attacks on American diplomatic missions in Libya and Egypt and by the death of an American consulate worker in Benghazi. It's disgraceful that the Obama Administration's first response was not to condemn attacks on our diplomatic missions, but to sympathize with those who waged the attacks.

The statement from Cairo was clearly unwise and later withdrawn, but it was not a 'first response' to the Benghazi attack, having been issued some 12 hours before the incident. It was another example of Romney's 'speak first, think later' approach. 'We screwed up, guys,' Romney told top aides on a conference call the following day.

Less than a week later, Romney was embroiled in another verbal gaffe as film of him addressing a Republican fundraiser emerged with Romney telling his audience:

> There are 47 percent of the people who will vote for the President no matter what, who are dependent upon government, who believe they are victims, and who believe the government has a responsibility to care for them, who believe that they are entitled to health care, to food, to housing, to you-name-it — that it's an entitlement and the government should give it to them. And they will vote for this president no matter what. My job is not to worry about those people. I'll never convince them they should take personal responsibility and care for their lives.

For a candidate who was fighting against a reputation of being rich, detached, aloof, unfeeling of ordinary Americans and gaffe-prone it merely gave further fuel to the fire and increased belief that Romney opens his mouth merely to change feet. It reinforced what his opponents were already saying about him — the most serious sort of political damage. 'If we had been speaking out about [poverty and its related issues] before this happened, it would have inoculated us a little bit,' said a Romney adviser. But they hadn't, so it didn't. And then came the television debates.

The television debates

With just under 5 weeks to go to Election Day, the first of the three presidential debates was held on 3 October. In *US Government & Politics* (Philip Allan Updates, 2013, 4th edition), I state that there are four rules of thumb about presidential debates and the first debate amply illustrated three of them. First, that 'style is often more important than substance'. While Governor Romney looked energetic, aggressive, engaged and positively enjoying the debate, President Obama looked uncharacteristically languid and disengaged, and appeared to be enduring rather than enjoying the occasion. In terms of 'style' Romney won the debate hands down. He even managed to look, dare one say it, 'presidential'.

A second rule of thumb is that debates 'are potentially more difficult for incumbents than challengers'. The main reason for this is that incumbent presidents have a record to defend. It's also true that just being on the same platform as the president of the United States gives the challenger a great advantage. For the first time, they address the nation (almost) as equals. Add to that the fact that there's more pressure on the president because he will always go into the debate as the clear favourite. So for him, expectations are higher. In this first debate that was also important because Obama was *unexpectedly* poor while Romney was *unexpectedly* good.

But there are some other good reasons why incumbents are at a disadvantage. Between June 2011 and February 2012, Governor Romney had participated in 19 debates with his Republican rivals. His debating skills were well practised. The last time President Obama had appeared in a televised debate was October 2008. As George Condon put it in his *National Journal* column ('Shaking the rust off', 29 September, 2012): 'Incumbents are almost always rusty when it comes to debating.' Furthermore, incumbent presidents have spent the last 4 years in the protective bubble of the Oval Office. True they have negotiated with foreign leaders, ordered military operations, consoled widows, managed budgets and the like, but they are entirely unused to being told for 90 minutes that they are a complete and utter failure and that their ideas are crackpot.

A third rule of thumb is that good sound bites are helpful. And here, Romney's were better than Obama's. 'Mr President,' said Governor Romney at one point, feeling he had been misrepresented, 'you're entitled as the president to your own airplane and to your own house, but not your own facts.' Romney talked about Obama's policy of 'trickle-down government' — a clever take on the accusation usually made by Democrats on Republicans of 'trickle-down economics'.

The result in the media and public opinion polls was remarkable. 'Romney, on offense, forces Obama to defend record', headlined the *Washington Post*. 'A president out of his depth', was Charles Hurt's headline in the *Washington Times*, while Joe Klein in *Time* magazine described Obama's appearance as 'one of the most inept performances by a president' in a television debate. The Gallup Poll which had Obama five points ahead of Romney (50–45) immediately before the debate had the race tied at 47–47 immediately afterwards. And those who viewed

Table 5.1 Regardless of which candidate you happen to support, who do you think did the better job in last night's debate?

	Romney (%)	Obama (%)	Both/Neither/No opinion (%)
All debate watchers	72	20	9
Republicans	97	2	1
Independents	70	19	11
Democrats	49	39	12

Source: **www.gallup.com**

the debate overwhelmingly believed that Romney did a better job than Obama, 72% to 20%. This 52 percentage point margin for a television debate winner was the largest that Gallup had ever recorded, beating the 42 point margin for Bill Clinton's win over President George H. W. Bush in the 1992 town hall television debate. What was even more extraordinary, as is shown in Table 5.1, was that even a majority of Democrats who watched the debate thought that Romney was the winner. A week later, Romney took the lead for the first time in the poll of polls compiled by the Real Clear Politics website (Figure 5.1).

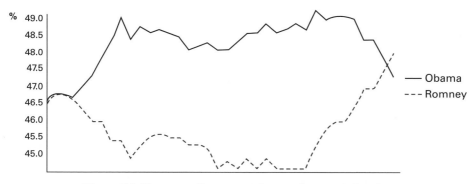

Figure 5.1 Obama vs Romney: 4 September to 10 October

Source: **www.realclearpolitics.com**

Obama, having studied the tape of the debate was angry with himself and for having let down his team. But the following week, Vice-President Biden put in a barnstorming performance in his debate with Congressman Paul Ryan. The remaining two presidential debates went pretty much to form with both candidates seemingly energised as the race entered its closing phase. The President was judged the winner in both, as well as over all three (Table 5.2), and Romney managed to negotiate them without committing any unpardonable gaffes.

The only trouble was that Romney was now sounding as if he were a completely different candidate from the one who had appeared thus far in the campaign. The 'severely conservative' Romney of the primaries and the earlier campaign had suddenly morphed into 'moderate Mitt'. To draw attention to this apparent

Table 5.2 Regardless of which candidate you happen to support, who do you think did the better job in last night's debate/all three debates?

Debate	Obama (%)	Romney (%)	Neither/Both (%)	Obama +/–
First	20	72	9	–52
Second	51	38	12	+13
Third	56	33	11	+23
All three	**46**	**44**	**10**	**+2**

Source: **www.gallup.com**

transformation, the President invented a new clinical condition — 'Romnesia' — from which he was convinced his opponent was suffering.

The swing states

Two weeks of campaigning remained after the final debate. By now it was all down to the so-called swing states — those that might swing into either the Obama column or the Romney column. On the day of the final debate, polls showed that out of eight swing states the President had a narrow lead in five, tied in two and Romney led in only one (Table 5.3). It was in these states that the election would be won or lost and it was here where enormous amounts of both time and money were expended in these final 2 weeks. The President would make five visits to both Ohio and Florida during this last fortnight as well as two each to Nevada and Colorado and one to each of Wisconsin, Iowa and Virginia. In one day alone — Thursday 25 October — the President visited five states, travelling 4,451 miles (Table 5.4).

During the same period, Governor Romney made seven visits to Ohio, five to Iowa, four to Florida, three to Virginia, two to New Hampshire and Nevada, plus one to each of Wisconsin, Colorado and rather inexplicably to Pennsylvania. But whereas the President would cover three, four or five states in a day, Romney's

Table 5.3 Average poll numbers in swing states, Monday 22 October

State	Obama (%)	Romney (%)	Obama +/–
Wisconsin	50	47	+3
Iowa	49	46	+3
Nevada	49	46	+3
Ohio	48	46	+2
New Hampshire	48	47	+1
Colorado	48	48	0
Virginia	48	48	0
Florida	47	49	–2

Source: **www.realclearpolitics.com**

US Government & Politics

Table 5.4 President Obama's schedule, Thursday 25 October

Travel route	Distance travelled (miles)
Las Vegas, Nevada, to Tampa, Florida	2,323
Tampa, Florida, to Richmond, Virginia	795
Richmond, Virginia, to Chicago, Illinois	617
Chicago, Illinois, to Cleveland, Ohio	345
Cleveland, Ohio, to Washington DC	371
Total	**4,451**

Source: **www.whitehouse.gov**

schedule was more sedate, often spending the whole day in one state, until the final 3 days when he made 11 stops in 7 different states.

There seemed little doubt, however, that the first debate had invigorated the Romney campaign. Crowds at Romney rallies were bigger and more exuberant. Indeed, the day after the first debate, the traffic was so bad for the Romney entourage trying to arrive at a venue in Fishersville, near Waynesboro, Virginia, that his aides thought there must have been a serious traffic accident. It turned out to be caused by the huge crowds of people trying to get to the Romney rally. And the polls were tightening, both in the nationwide head-to-head with the President and in a number of the swing states. By Sunday 28 October, Romney had led the President in the Real Clear Politics poll-of-polls on 17 of the previous 20 days. But there was still just time for Romney to be blown off course — quite literally.

The storm

On Monday 22 October, the day of the final presidential debate, a tropical depression formed in the western Caribbean. Two days later it was upgraded to a hurricane and, being the eighteenth named Atlantic storm of the 2012 season, was christened 'Sandy'. During the next seven days, Sandy visited its wrath on Jamaica, Haiti, Cuba and the Dominican Republic. It then swept up the eastern seaboard of the USA before making a sharp left turn to come ashore over the Mid-Atlantic and North-eastern states with New Jersey and New York feeling its full impact just 8 days before Election Day. In the USA alone, Sandy would claim over 100 lives and cause something like $50 billion worth of damage.

One might suggest that it also claimed one politician's life too — that of Governor Romney. It stopped his momentum in its tracks, wiped him off the television news and front pages for days and relegated him to handling soup cans and bottled water while the President met with his emergency team in the Situation Room of the White House in the full glare of the national media. This was the 'October Surprise' to end all October surprises. All it needed now was for a highly-respected Republican politician, in the form of Governor Chris Christie, the Republican governor of New Jersey, to step up and say what a great job the President was doing.

Christie, who had been one of the President's sharpest critics, was now in front of the television cameras saying that Obama's response to Sandy had been 'outstanding' and that he could not 'thank the President enough for his personal concern and compassion for our state'. Seeing the two indulge in a warm public handshake, Mitt Romney must have turned in his political grave. Six days later, the President was re-elected to a second term.

Questions

1 What verbal gaffes did Romney commit during the campaign?
2 How did Romney's performance in the first television debate illustrate three of the four rules of thumb about these debates?
3 What do Figure 5.1 and Table 5.1 show about the effect of the first debate?
4 Analyse Obama's and Romney's travel schedule during the final 2 weeks of the campaign.
5 What effect did Hurricane Sandy play in the final days of the campaign?

Chapter 6

Why Obama won: analysing the vote

Put simply, Mitt Romney blew it. This was an election that the incumbent president should have lost. With the economy — by far and away voters' number one issue — still bumping along the bottom and showing few signs of a fast or sustained recovery, gas (petrol) prices soaring to nearly $4 a gallon, a bundle of broken promises from 4 years before, and the majority of voters believing the country was 'pretty seriously off on the wrong track', this looked a lot more like the elections of 1980 and 1992 when incumbent presidents Jimmy Carter and George H. W. Bush lost, than like 1996 and 2004 when Bill Clinton and George W. Bush were re-elected.

But when all was said and done, President Obama *was* re-elected with just shy of 51% of the popular vote, winning 332 Electoral College votes to Romney's 206. For all the media talk of a race that was too close to call, in the end Obama was home and dry with a 62-vote margin of comfort in the Electoral College. He could have lost Florida, Ohio and Virginia with their 60 electoral votes and still been re-elected. Romney did not just lose, he gained fewer votes than the losers in both the previous elections — nearly 1.5 million fewer than John McCain in 2008, and nearly 0.5 million fewer than John Kerry in 2004. Only two states switched party control from 2008 — Indiana and North Carolina, both from Obama to the Republicans.

However, Obama was re-elected with a lower Electoral College vote and a lower percentage of the popular vote than in his first election, and this is highly unusual as Table 6.1 shows. Most presidents running for re-election are voted back with a bigger majority than they had before, or else they lose. Obama was the first president since Woodrow Wilson in 1916 to be re-elected with a smaller number of Electoral College votes and the first since Ulysses Grant in 1872 to be re-elected to a consecutive second term with a smaller share of the popular vote than first time around. So before we consider the reasons why Obama won, let us briefly look at why this was an election which he should really have lost and why therefore it is true to say that Romney blew it.

Why Obama should have lost

'What ought to pain Republicans most about Barack Obama's victory is that 2012 was entirely winnable for them,' wrote Jacob Weisberg in the *Financial Times* the day after the election. There are four reasons worth considering which suggested this was an election President Obama would lose.

Table 6.1 First and second elections compared, 1912–2012

President	% of popular vote		Result	Difference in popular vote
	1st election	2nd election		
Woodrow Wilson	41.9	49.3	Won	Up 7.6
Herbert Hoover	58.2	39.7	Lost	Down 18.5
Franklin Roosevelt	57.4	60.8	Won	Up 3.4
Dwight Eisenhower	55.1	57.4	Won	Up 2.3
Richard Nixon	43.6	60.7	Won	Up 17.1
Jimmy Carter	50.0	41.0	Lost	Down 9.0
Ronald Reagan	50.7	58.8	Won	Up 8.1
George H. W. Bush	53.4	37.4	Lost	Down 16.0
Bill Clinton	42.3	49.2	Won	Up 6.9
George W. Bush	47.9	53.2	Won	Up 5.3
Barack Obama	52.9	50.5	Won	Down 2.4

The state of the US economy

By far and away the most important was the state of the US economy. When Barack Obama came to the White House in January 2009, unemployment in the USA stood at 7.8%. By October of that year it had reached 10%. At the time of the mid-term elections in November 2010 it was still 9.8%. True it was down to 7.9% by the time of the 2012 election, but unemployment was still higher than it was in 1976 when President Ford lost, higher than it was in 1980 when President Carter lost, and higher than it was in 1992 when the first President Bush lost. As Table 6.2 shows, no president in recent times had been re-elected with unemployment higher than 7.3%.

Folk who filled their car with petrol to travel to Washington DC in January 2009 for Barack Obama's first inaugural would have paid a national average of $1.89

Table 6.2 Unemployment at time of elections featuring an incumbent president, 1976–2012

President	Year	Unemployment rate (%)	Won/lost election
Bill Clinton	1996	5.2	Won
George W. Bush	2004	5.4	Won
Ronald Reagan	1984	7.3	Won
Jimmy Carter	1980	7.5	Lost
George H. W. Bush	1992	7.6	Lost
Gerald Ford	1976	7.6	Lost
Barack Obama	**2012**	**7.9**	**Won**

Source: US Bureau of Labor Statistics

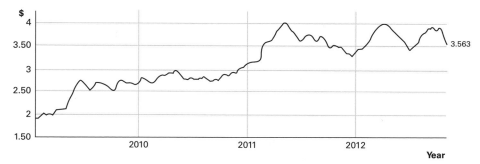

Figure 6.1 US average retail gasoline (petrol) price, 2009–12

Source: www.tinyurl.com/bss5zkf

a gallon. By April 2012 a gallon cost just shy of $4 and it was still at $3.91 in October, a month before Election Day (Figure 6.1). That would normally spell disaster for an incumbent president.

Neither were voters confident of the President's stewardship of the economy. When asked in October, 'Do you approve or disapprove of President Obama's handling of the economy?' 47% said they approved but 52% said they disapproved. Again, here was fertile ground for a challenger in a presidential election. In an election in which exit polls showed 77% of voters thought the state of the economy was 'not so good or poor', the incumbent really should have been on the losing side. But Obama managed to get 38% of the vote among these voters while winning 90% among the 23% of voters who thought the economy was 'excellent or good'.

Obama's approval rating

Another useful indicator of an incumbent president's chances of re-election is his approval rating. History shows us that it is exceedingly difficult for a president to be re-elected going into that election with an approval rating below 50%. Table 6.3 shows the last eight presidents seeking re-election with their respective

Table 6.3 Presidential approval ratings during the 14th quarter, 1956–2012

President	Date (May–July)	14th quarter approval rating (%)	Won/lost re-election
Dwight Eisenhower	1956	70.8	Won
Richard Nixon	1972	57.8	Won
Bill Clinton	1996	55.2	Won
Ronald Reagan	1984	53.9	Won
George W. Bush	2004	47.9	Won
Barack Obama	**2012**	**46.8**	**Won**
George H. W. Bush	1992	39.2	Lost
Jimmy Carter	1980	35.8	Lost

Source: www.gallup.com

approval ratings between May and July of election year — the 14th quarter of their presidencies. Obama's 46.8% put him below the five presidents who were re-elected, but above the two who were defeated. The Gallup poll conducted between the fifth and seventh of November (Election Day was the sixth) still showed the President's approval rating at just 49%.

The right track/wrong track question

Not only did the economy and his approval ratings make President Obama vulnerable, but so did the fact that the majority of Americans believed the country to be 'pretty seriously off on the wrong track' rather than 'generally going in the right direction'. This right track/wrong track question is another usually reliable guide to a president's re-election chances. If the right-trackers are in the majority — as in 1996 and 2004 — then the president is re-elected, but if the wrong-trackers are in the majority — as in 1992 — then the president is defeated (Table 6.4).

Table 6.4 Right track/wrong track polls: 1992, 1996, 2004 and 2012

	1992 Bush I	1996 Clinton	2004 Bush II	2012 Obama
Right track	22%	**53%**	**49%**	46%
Wrong track	**76%**	43%	46%	**52%**
Result	Lost	Won	Won	Won

You don't need a political science degree to work out the logic of this. Surely, if you believe the country is on the wrong track, you will cast your vote to change direction — that is vote for the challenger. Why on earth would you vote for 4 more years on the wrong track? As Figure 6.2 shows, the wrong trackers had been in the majority for the entire 4 years of Obama's first term. Even the 2012 Election Day exit poll showed the wrong trackers in the majority — 46% to 52%. Of the 52% who thought the country was on the wrong track, 84% voted for Governor Romney. Here was another factor which Romney should have been able to exploit.

Obama's broken promises

Finally, there were Obama's broken promises — nowhere more obvious than in the fact that the detention camp at Guantanamo Bay remained open for business

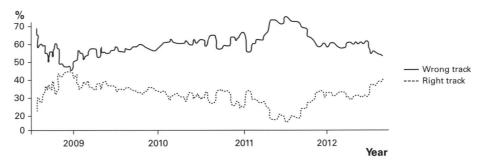

Figure 6.2 Right track/wrong track, 2009–12

Source: **www.realclearpolitics.com**

despite the President having signed an executive order on his first day in office to close it. Where was the 'change we can believe in' from the first campaign? Where was 'the audacity of hope'? Where was the confidence — and evidence — of 'Yes we can!'? Yet for all this, Romney could prise only two states away from the President and fell 64 votes short in the Electoral College. So why did Obama win?

Why Obama won — again

The 2012 presidential election results by state, showing the change in the Democratic vote from 2008, are listed in Table 6.5. There are six reasons we can consider to explain why President Obama won in 2012 (Box 6.1).

Box 6.1	**Six reasons why Obama won — again**

1. Incumbency and a united party
2. Early attacks on Romney
3. Running the better campaign
4. Romney — the man and the gaffes
5. Two former presidents
6. An October surprise

He was the incumbent

First — the much overlooked but critically important reason — he was the incumbent. Since 1796, 31 presidents have run for re-election: 22 of them have won; only 9 have lost. Only five sitting presidents lost re-election races in the twentieth century — Taft (1912), Hoover (1932), Ford (1976), Carter (1980) and the first George Bush (1992). But Ford had never been elected to office so only four elected presidents had failed to win re-election in the past 100 years. Add to that, Obama faced no significant primary challenge (see Chapter 2). Trying to defeat an incumbent president with a united party behind him is well-nigh impossible. Ford, Carter and Bush all faced significant opposition in the primaries in their re-election years. Obama did not. Whoever had taken on Obama, this would have been a formidable mountain to climb.

His early advantage

This leads to a second reason — Obama's brilliant use of his early advantage. Obama used the same tactics against Romney that President Clinton had used against Bob Dole in 1996 and that President Bush had used against John Kerry in 2004. Before Romney could introduce himself to the national electorate as the Republican nominee, the Obama folk defined the former chief executive of Bain Capital as 'a tax-dodging, job-outsourcing villain who would shred the safety net holding up the elderly and the poor' (Beth Reinhard, 'How Obama won', *National Journal,* 7 November).

This was done mostly in a blizzard of negative television ads aired in swing states. 'I think they were very smart in defining him early. The ads paid off,' commented Rick Tyler, a Republican strategist. 'I don't think he ever really recovered.' So in the third week of July, while Romney was off on his less than successful European tour, the Democrats were spending $1.2 million on negative ads which played

Table 6.5 2012 presidential election results by state, showing change in the Democratic vote from 2008

State	Obama vote (%)	Romney vote (%)	Change in Democrat vote from 2008 (%)	Electoral College votes	
				Obama (D)	Romney (R)
Alabama	38	61	−1		9
Alaska	42	54	+3		3
Arizona	44	54	−1		11
Arkansas	37	61	−2		6
California	60	38	−1	55	
Colorado	51	46	−2	9	
Connecticut	58	41	−2	7	
Delaware	59	40	−2	3	
Florida	50	49	−1	29	
Georgia	45	53	−2		16
Hawaii	71	28	−1	4	
Idaho	33	65	−3		4
Illinois	57	41	−5	20	
Indiana	**44**	**54**	**−6**		**11**
Kansas	38	60	−3		6
Kentucky	38	61	−3		8
Louisiana	41	59	+1		8
Maine	56	41	−2	4	
Maryland	61	37	0	10	
Massachusetts	61	38	−1	11	
Michigan	54	45	−3	16	
Minnesota	53	45	−1	10	
Mississippi	44	56	+1		6
Missouri	44	54	−5		10
Montana	42	56	−5		3
Nebraska	38	60	−3		5
Nevada	52	46	−3	6	
New Hampshire	52	46	−2	4	

New Jersey	58	41	+1	14	
New Mexico	53	43	−4	5	
New York	63	36	+1	29	
North Carolina	**48**	**50**	**−2**		**15**
North Dakota	39	58	−6		3
Ohio	50	48	−1	18	
Oklahoma	33	67	−1		7
Oregon	54	43	−3	7	
Pennsylvania	52	47	−3	20	
Rhode Island	63	35	0	4	
South Carolina	44	55	−1		9
South Dakota	40	58	−5		3
Tennessee	39	59	−3		11
Texas	41	57	−3		38
Vermont	67	31	0	3	
Virginia	51	48	−1	13	
Washington	56	42	−2	12	
West Virginia	36	62	−7		5
Wisconsin	53	46	−3	10	
Wyoming	28	69	−5		3
District of Columbia	91	7	−2	3	
Totals	**51**	**48**	**−2**	**332**	**206**

Republican gains from 2008 in **bold**

1,947 times on Ohio television stations alone. *Firms* first aired on 14 July. It was used in all eight swing states and accused Romney of 'shipping companies to China, jobs to India and his personal wealth to tax havens in Bermuda'. 'Mitt Romney's not the solution. He's the problem,' intoned the narrator at the close. (You can watch this television ad at **www.livingroomcandidate.org**) Talking after the election, a Romney adviser commented:

> If we were to go back and change one thing, we'd spend more money and more strongly defend Mitt and push back on the 'rich guy' issue, the Bain Capital issue. We should have done more positive ads to get his favourables up.

But they did nothing and Romney's poll numbers fell. As a result, an election which should have been a referendum on Barack Obama's economic stewardship turned into a referendum on Mitt Romney's character.

He ran the better campaign

This leads directly to a third reason for Obama's victory — that he ran by far the better campaign in terms of voter registration, organisation, use of money and get-out-the-vote effort. As Democratic strategist Joe Trippi commented: 'The Obama campaign knew they weren't supposed to get re-elected, so they figured out who they needed to register to vote and turn out to change that.' An incumbent president who has not had to be out campaigning in primaries and caucuses earlier in the year might be thought to be at a disadvantage to his challenger who has. But the Obama campaign started early and was always ahead in terms of organisation by carefully maintaining its superb precinct-level ground game from 2008.

By the spring of 2012, Obama had more field offices open than all his potential Republican rivals put together. This was especially critical in key swing states. By the summer, while Romney had 52 offices open across Florida, Obama had 106; Romney had 40 offices in Ohio, but the President had 131. Vice-President Joe Biden visiting Colorado 2 days before Election Day told volunteers that 'the ground operation which you guys represent is the best in the history of presidential politics,' and though not impartial, Biden may well have been right. On Election Day, the African-American share of the vote in Ohio jumped from 11% in 2008 to 15%. In Florida, the Hispanic share of the vote jumped from 14% in 2008 to 17%. Ninety-six percent of African-Americans in Ohio and 60% of Hispanics in Florida voted for the President.

Mitt Romney himself

A fourth reason for Obama's victory was Mitt Romney himself — the man and the gaffes. Mitt Romney was never going to be someone who could effortlessly and easily communicate with ordinary voters. He lacks the common touch of a Ronald Reagan, a Bill Clinton or a George W. Bush. Moreover, his moderate political philosophy made him ill-suited to attract the enthusiastic support of social conservatives, and his Mormon faith sat awkwardly with evangelical Christians — two important voting blocs for any Republican presidential candidate.

Although since his abortive campaign in 2008 he had swapped his business suits for blue jeans, in the words of Lisa Lerer ('Romney lost race in summer after Obama defined résumé,' **www.bloomberg.com**, 7 November 2012) 'in factories and fast-food restaurants, he was an awkward presence uneasy at making small-talk with voters.' He still looked like the quintessential Brylcreemed executive, someone who was uncomfortable discussing his personal wealth, estimated at around $250 million. He was in many ways the Republicans' answer to John Kerry — the super-wealthy Massachusetts senator who lost to George W. Bush in 2004.

Then there were the mistakes made during the campaign. The *Oxford English Dictionary* has named 'omnishambles' as its Word of the Year for 2012. Maybe its US counterpart should make room for 'Romneyshambles'. According to Republican strategist John Brabender, Romney and his team 'forgot they had to give people a reason to vote *for* Romney, not just *against* Obama'. Romney badly misread the electorate, assuming that a faltering economy would automatically send voters running to support his campaign. Then there were the verbal gaffes (Box 6.2) — the most damaging of which was the 47% remark secretly filmed at a Romney fundraiser. Even when it was publicised, Romney failed to apologise, saying merely that 'the response has not been elegantly stated'. It was another 3 weeks before he fully disavowed the remark and apologised.

Having run so far to the right during the Republican primaries, Romney left it far too late to return to the centre and to portray the picture of 'moderate Mitt' rather than 'severely conservative' Mitt. And when the makeover came — in the final month of the campaign — voters couldn't then figure out which was the real Mitt Romney, and if they voted for him and he won, which Romney would show up in the Oval Office. So by the time of his strong performance in the first debate, in the view of *National Journal's* Michael Hirsh, 'it was too late to overcome an image of incompetence, aloofness and lack of definition'.

Help from his two predecessors

A fifth reason for Obama's victory was the help he received from his two predecessors. Bill Clinton proved to be a most effective campaigner for Obama — even after all the bitterness between them 4 years before. Clinton gave an impressive speech at the Democratic convention articulating more clearly than even Obama himself why the President should be re-elected. He featured in television ads urging people to vote for Obama and campaigned tirelessly and effectively for him.

But as Table 6.6 shows, Obama also received some significant help — though more indirectly — from George W. Bush. When exit pollsters asked who voters thought

Table 6.6 Exit poll question: 'Who is more to blame for current economic problems: Barack Obama or George W. Bush?

	Total (%)	Voted for Obama (%)	Voted for Romney (%)
Barack Obama	38	5	94
George W. Bush	53	85	12

was more to blame for the USA's current economic problems, a majority named George W. Bush, with only 38% laying the blame at Obama's door. This was quite remarkable, the more so as no one as far as I know ever heard Obama name his predecessor as the cause of the country's economic woes. And of the 53% who blamed Bush, 85% voted for Obama while of the 38% who blamed Obama, 94% voted for Romney.

The 'October surprise'

Finally, there was the most extraordinary 'October surprise'. An October surprise is an unexpected development or event so late in the campaign that the side it disadvantages does not have time to adequately respond to it before Election Day. Previous October surprises include the indictment of the former secretary of defense Caspar Weinberger on matters relating to the Iran-Contra affair 4 days before the 1992 election, and the press disclosure 5 days before the 2000 election that George W. Bush had paid a $150 fine following a drink-driving incident 24 years earlier.

In 2012, the October surprise came in the shape of Hurricane Sandy which wreaked havoc in the mid-Atlantic and the North-east, especially in the states of New Jersey and New York. The hurricane stopped Romney's momentum and took him out of the headline news for at least three critical days while allowing the President to play the roles of commander- and comforter-in-chief. When the Republican governor of New Jersey Chris Christie publicly described the President's actions as 'outstanding', the media began to talk about a possible 'Sandy effect' on the race. As Table 6.5 shows, New Jersey and New York were two of only five states in which Obama increased his share of the vote from 2008. And as Table 6.7 shows, 64% of voters said that Obama's response to the hurricane was a factor in their voting and almost two-thirds of those voted for Obama, with only 36% choosing Romney. Exit polls also showed Obama winning 50–45 among the 6% of voters who decided 'in the last few days' and by 51–44 among the 3% who decided on Election Day. Late deciders broke for the President.

Who voted for whom in 2012?

Table 6.8 shows a breakdown of who voted for whom and, where possible, compares the figures in each category with voting in 2008. With a few notable exceptions, the table shows clearly that Obama lost support pretty much across the board. First we consider the two most interesting voting groups — those relating to gender and race.

Table 6.7 Exit poll question: 'In your vote for president, how would you rate the importance of Obama's hurricane response?'

	Total (%)	Voted for Obama (%)	Voted for Romney (%)
A factor	64	62	36
Not a factor	31	28	70

Table 6.8 Who voted for whom? 2012 and 2008 compared

Category	2012		2008		Change in Dem vote since 2008
	Obama (%)	Romney (%)	Obama (%)	McCain (%)	
All (100)	51	48	53	46	−2
Men (47)	45	52	49	48	−4
Women (53)	55	44	56	43	−1
Whites (72)	39	59	43	55	−4
African Americans (13)	93	6	95	4	−2
Hispanics/Latinos (10)	71	27	67	31	+4
Asian (3)	73	26	62	35	+11
White men (34)	35	62	41	57	−6
White women (38)	42	56	46	53	−4
Black men (5)	87	11	95	5	−8
Black women (8)	96	3	96	3	0
Hispanic/Latino men (5)	65	33	64	33	+1
Hispanic/Latino women (6)	76	23	68	30	+8
Aged 18–29 (19)	60	37	66	32	−6
Aged 30–44 (27)	52	45	52	46	0
Aged 45–64 (38)	47	51	–	–	–
Aged 65+ (16)	44	56	–	–	–
All Protestant (53)	42	57	45	54	−3
White Protestant (39)	30	69	34	65	−4
White evangelicals (26)	21	78	24	74	−3
Catholic (25)	50	48	54	45	−4
Jewish (2)	69	30	78	21	−9
Mormon (2)	21	78	–	–	–
Attend religious services:					
Weekly (42)	39	39	39	55	−4
Occasionally (40)	55	55	55	42	−2
Never (17)	62	62	62	30	−5

(Continued)

Table 6.8 Who voted for whom? 2012 and 2008 compared (Continued)

Category	2012		2008		Change in Dem vote since 2008
	Obama (%)	Romney (%)	Obama (%)	McCain (%)	
Population of area:					
Over 500,000 (11)	**69**	29	70	28	−1
50,000 to 500,000 (21)	**58**	40	59	39	−1
Suburbs (47)	48	**50**	50	48	−2
Small town (8)	42	**56**	45	53	−3
Rural (14)	37	**61**	45	53	−8
Democrats (38)	**92**	7	89	10	+3
Republicans (32)	6	**93**	9	90	−3
Independents (29)	45	**50**	52	44	−7
Liberal (25)	**86**	11	89	10	−3
Moderate (41)	**56**	41	60	39	−4
Conservatives (35)	17	**82**	20	78	−3
Family income:					
Under $30,000 (20)	**63**	35	–	–	–
$30–49,999 (21)	**57**	42	55	43	+2
$50–99,999 (31)	46	**52**	–	–	–
$100–199,999 (21)	44	**54**	48	51	−4
$200–249,99 (3)	47	**52**	–	–	–
Over $250,000 (4)	42	**55**	–	–	–

Winner in **bold**

Gender

Obama's vote among men was down 4 percentage points from 2008, with Romney winning the male vote by 7 points. But Obama held an 11-point advantage among women who yet again comprised a larger proportion of the electorate than did men. This double-digit advantage among a group which made up 53% of voters was highly significant in determining the result.

With the Republican Party in general and Romney in particular — at least for much of the campaign — taking issue positions which were unattractive to the majority of women, it was in some ways surprising that Obama's advantage was not larger. For many women, the Republican Party simply could not pass the credibility test and just when Romney might have made progress among female voters, up popped Republican Senate candidates like Todd Akin in Missouri and Richard Mourdock in Indiana to remind women what they found so repugnant about the Republican Party on gender issues.

Race

To misquote Sherlock Holmes, this was clearly the dog that *did* bark in this election as immigration joined abortion as another wedge issue which the Democrats cleverly used to their advantage. With Romney suggesting that the answer to illegal immigration was 'self-deportation', it was hardly surprising that the Republican share of the ever-growing Hispanic vote fell yet again. Back in 2004, President Bush won the votes of 43% of Hispanic voters. Four years later, after McCain's lurch to the right on immigration, the Hispanic Republican vote was down to 31%. Romney managed to get it down another 4 points in 2012. Yet during the same period the proportion of voters who were Hispanic increased from 6% to 10%. As many Hispanics would describe themselves as conservatives, they ought to be easily attracted to support Republican candidates. Not only did Obama increase his Hispanic support by 4 points from 2008, but his support among Asians increased by a staggering 11 points.

The Republican Party used to be able to win elections by merely chalking up a reasonable majority among white voters. When Ronald Reagan beat President Carter back in 1980 (489–49 in the Electoral College), Reagan won just 56% of the white vote — that's less than the 59% of the white vote which Romney gained in 2012 and he lost 206–332 in the Electoral College. The crucial difference is that in 1980, white voters accounted for 88% of the electorate. By 2012 they accounted for just 72%. That figure has fallen in each of the last six elections as Table 6.9 shows. Just 20 years ago, whites made up 87% of the electorate. Although Romney gained a higher percentage of the white vote than any candidate over these six elections, it was insufficient to get him over the winning line. We must therefore presume that the Republican Party must expand its support among minority voters if it is to win future elections.

Table 6.9 The white vote won by Republican candidates, 1992–2012

Year	Voters who were white (%)	Republican candidate	Republican share of white vote (%)
1992	87	George H. W. Bush	39
1996	83	Bob Dole	45
2000	82	George W. Bush	54
2004	77	George W. Bush	58
2008	74	John McCain	55
2012	72	**Mitt Romney**	59

Other trends

- Despite forecasts to the contrary, **young voters** (18–29-year-olds) made up a larger proportion of the electorate than in 2008 and although their level of support for Obama fell by 6 points, the turnout of young voters was important to Obama's victory.
- The **suburbs** have long been regarded as the bellwether of the US electorate. In all eight elections between 1980 and 2008, suburbanites voted for the winner — but not in 2012, with Romney winning this group by 2 percentage points.

- In seven of the last eight elections, self-identifying **independent voters** had also voted for the winner — 2004 being the only exception when Kerry won that group by 1 point. But in 2012, Romney won among independents, and by 5 points.
- **White evangelical voters** made up 26% of the electorate, the same as in 2008, and Romney's vote was up 4 percentage points among this group compared with 4 years ago. There was therefore no obvious Mormon effect in 2012.

Table 6.10 shows the answers to six significant questions asked in the exit poll. Clearly the economy was by far and away voters' most important issue. True Mitt

Table 6.10 Voting and issues, 2012

Issues	Obama (%)	Romney (%)
Which one of these issues is the most important facing the country?		
• The economy (59)	47	**51**
• Healthcare (18)	**75**	24
• Federal budget deficit (15)	32	**66**
• Foreign policy (5)	**56**	33
Which one of these candidate qualities mattered most in deciding how you voted for president?		
• Has a vision for the future (29)	45	**54**
• Shares my values (27)	42	**55**
• Cares about people like me (21)	**81**	18
• Is a strong leader (18)	38	**61**
Should income tax rates:		
• Increase for all (13)	**52**	44
• Increase only on income over $250,000 (47)	**70**	29
• Not increase for anyone (35)	23	**75**
What should happen to the 2010 healthcare law?		
• Expand it (26)	**92**	5
• Leave it as it is (18)	**80**	19
• Repeal some of it (24)	27	**72**
• Repeal all of it (25)	3	**93**
Should most illegal immigrants working in the United States be:		
• Offered a chance to apply for legal status (65)	**61**	37
• Deported to the country they came from (28)	24	**73**
Which is closer to your view:		
• Government should do more to solve problems (43)	**81**	17
• Government is doing too many things already (51)	24	**74**

Winner in **bold**

Romney won among the 59% of voters who named this as their most important issue. But, as we discussed earlier, given the state of the economy, one would have expected Romney to have won this group of voters by more than 4 points and thereby won the election. So how did Obama manage to gain the votes of 47% of those who viewed the economy as their most important issue? Polling by the Benenson Strategy Group found that 74% of voters said that what the country had faced since 2008 was 'an extraordinary crisis, more severe than we've seen in decades', while only 23% thought it was 'a typical recession that the country sees every few years'. Furthermore, 57% of voters believed the crisis was 'too severe for anyone to fix in a single [presidential] term' and only four out of ten voters believed that another president would have been able to have done more to get the economy moving in the previous 4 years.

Not only did Romney lead on the most important issue, but he also led on the top two candidate qualities — vision and values — which is not what one would expect the loser to do. It also remains something of a mystery to me how Romney won on either vision or values, let alone on being 'a strong leader'. Abraham Lincoln was clearly right that 'you can fool some of the people all of the time'. That said, Obama was clearly in tune with the majority of voters in advocating that the wealthiest Americans should pay more in income tax while the anti-tax advocates sided with Governor Romney.

The last three questions in Table 6.10 show the polarising nature of 'Obamacare', immigration and the role of the federal government with people's views on these issues clearly defining how they cast their votes. However, it is worth noting — and the Republican Party certainly needs to — that whereas the nation is fairly evenly split on Obamacare and the role of the federal government, there is a clear majority in favour of positive immigration reform as opposed to deportation of illegal immigrants.

Conclusion

The post mortems for the Republican Party in general and the Romney campaign in particular will continue well into 2013. But the Republicans have now lost the popular vote in five out of the last six presidential elections and in those elections — from 1992 through 2012 — they averaged only 45% of the popular vote and 210 Electoral College votes. In the previous six elections — from 1968 through 1988 — the Republicans averaged 53% of the popular vote and 417 Electoral College votes. Indeed, their lowest electoral vote total during that earlier period was 240 (Ford, 1976) — 30 more than the average in the more recent period. And their highest popular vote total in the last six elections was just under 51%, well below the average for the previous six elections. Put simply, you do not win presidential elections with 45% of the popular vote and 210 votes in the Electoral College.

The Republicans must also face the implications of the declining white vote and the increasing 'brown' vote of African Americans, Hispanics and Asians. Both their candidates and their policies — and not just on immigration — need to be more attractive to minority voters. This was also the seventh consecutive election in which the Republicans lost the female vote. Over these seven elections — 1988 through 2012 — the Republican vote among women has averaged just 43% compared with over 52% for the Democrats.

Obama has become the third consecutive two-term president, following Bill Clinton (1993–2001) and George W. Bush (2001–09). This is the first time the USA has had three consecutive two-term presidents since Jefferson, Madison and Monroe followed each other between 1800 and 1820. But now Obama's challenge begins. He will need to come up with a vision for the next 4 years which seemed to so elude him during the campaign and find some way of working with a divided and partisan Congress. Given the record of previous second terms, he may soon come to wonder why he fought so hard to win one.

Questions

1 In what ways was Obama's re-election result unusual?
2 Using the data in Tables 6.2, 6.3 and 6.4 as well as in Figures 6.1 and 6.2, explain why Obama should have lost this election.
3 How important is incumbency in presidential elections?
4 What were Obama's early advantages and how did he put them to good use?
5 In what ways did Obama run the better campaign?
6 To what extent and in what ways was Romney responsible for losing the race?
7 How did Obama receive help from his two immediate predecessors?
8 Explain the term 'October surprise' and its effect on the 2012 race.
9 Why did Obama win the majority of the female vote?
10 What problems do the Republicans face regarding white and non-white voters? Refer to the data shown in Table 6.9.
11 What do the data in Table 6.10 tell us about voting and issues?
12 How did the polling by the Benenson Strategy Group help explain Obama's re-election in the face of economic woes?
13 What future challenges face (a) the Republican Party and (b) President Obama?

Chapter 7

The congressional races: more divided government

In the 2012 congressional races, 33 Senate seats and all 435 House seats were up for election.

In the **Senate**, of the 33 seats — those last contested in 2006 — 23 were defended by Democrats and only 10 by Republicans. Ten senators retired — 7 Democrats and only 3 Republicans. Those figures made it look very likely that the Republicans would make the overall gain of just 4 seats they needed to win back the majority. The big surprise, therefore, was that it was the Democrats who made gains in these elections — losing in Nebraska but gaining seats in Indiana, Massachusetts and, in effect, in Maine where independent Angus King will caucus with the Democrats, replacing Republican Olympia Snowe (Table 7.1). The Democrats

Table 7.1 Results of Senate elections, 2012

State	Winner	Party	%	Opponent(s)	Party	%
Arizona	Rep. Jeff Flake*	R	50	Richard Carmona	D	45
California	**Dianne Feinstein**	D	61	Elizabeth Emken	R	39
Connecticut	Rep. Chris Murphy*	D	55	Linda McMahon	R	43
Delaware	**Tom Carper**	D	66	Kevin Wade	R	29
Florida	**Bill Nelson**	D	55	Rep. Connie Mack IV	R	42
Hawaii	Rep. Mazie Hirono*	D	63	Ex-Gov. Linda Lingle	R	37
Indiana	Rep. Joe Donnelly	D	50	Richard Mourdock*	R	44
Maine	Ex-Gov. Angus King	Ind	53	Charles Summers*	R	30
				Cynthia Dill	D	13
Maryland	**Ben Cardin**	D	54	Dan Bongino	R	28
Massachusetts	Elizabeth Warren	D	54	**Scott Brown**	R	46
Michigan	**Debbie Stabenow**	D	58	Ex-Rep. Pete Hoekstra	R	39
Minnesota	**Amy Klobuchar**	D	65	State Rep. Kurt Bills	R	30
Mississippi	**Roger Wicker**	R	57	Albert Gore	D	40
Missouri	**Claire McCaskill**	D	55	Rep. Todd Akin	R	39
Montana	**Jon Tester**	D	49	Denny Rehberg	R	48
Nebraska	Deb Fischer	R	58	Ex-Sen. Bob Kerrey*	D	42
Nevada	**Dean Heller**	R	46	Shelley Berkley	D	45
New Jersey	**Bob Menendez**	D	58	Joe Kyrillos	R	40
New Mexico	Martin Heinrich*	D	51	Ex-Rep. Heather Wilson	R	45
New York	**Kirsten Gillibrand**	D	72	Wendy Long	R	27

(Continued)

Table 7.1 Results of Senate elections, 2012 (Continued)

State	Winner	Party	%	Opponent(s)	Party	%
North Dakota	Heidi Heitkamp*	D	51	Rick Berg	R	49
Ohio	**Sherrod Brown**	D	50	Josh Mandel	R	45
Pennsylvania	**Bob Casey**	D	54	Tom Smith	R	45
Rhode Island	**Sheldon Whitehouse**	D	65	Barry Hinckley	R	35
Tennessee	**Bob Corker**	R	65	Mark Clayton	D	30
Texas	Ted Cruz*	R	57	Paul Sadler	D	41
Utah	**Orrin Hatch**	R	65	Scott Howell	D	30
Vermont	**Bernie Sanders**	Ind	71	John MacGovern	R	25
Virginia	Ex-Gov. Tim Kaine*	D	52	Ex-Sen. George Allen	R	48
Washington	**Maria Cantwell**	D	59	Michael Baumgartner	R	41
West Virginia	**Joe Manchin**	D	61	John Raese	R	37
Wisconsin	Rep. Tammy Baldwin*	D	52	Ex-Gov. Tommy Thompson	R	46
Wyoming	**John Barrasso**	R	76	Tim Chesnut	D	22

Bold = incumbent

* = incumbent party in open seat

thereby increased their margin from 53–47 to 55–45. The other headline was the fact that the new Senate would include 20 women — up from 17 in 2011–12 — with five of the twelve new senators being women, 4 Democrats and 1 Republican.

The two races the Republicans virtually threw away were those in Indiana and Missouri. In Indiana, the Republican incumbent Richard Lugar was defeated in the primary but the winner of that race, Tea Party favourite Richard Mourdock, went on to lose in the general election after making a crass and offensive remark about rape. In Missouri, Democrat incumbent Claire McCaskill was initially given little or no chance of holding her seat — until, that is, the Republicans in their primary chose another Tea Party favourite Todd Akin. He self-destructed with a comment about 'legitimate rape' and McCaskill went on to a 16 percentage-point win in November. Thus two poor candidates cost the Republicans two winnable seats. They also lost with strong(er) candidates in Connecticut, Florida, Hawaii, Massachusetts, New Mexico, Virginia and Wisconsin — all races they had at one time thought they could realistically win. Their dismal performance was shown by the fact that the average vote for Republican challengers was a paltry 39% while the average vote for Democrat winners was 57%.

In the **House of Representatives** these were the first elections held after the reapportionment following the 2010 census. A number of states had gained or lost one or more House seats and new district boundaries were therefore in operation in many states, making like-for-like comparisons with the 2010 elections quite difficult. It also meant that in some districts both candidates were incumbents — either in the primary or in the general election. Thirteen incumbents — eight Democrats and six Republicans — were defeated in the primaries including eight in incumbent vs incumbent races. The five who lost to challengers were Tim Holden (D-Pa 17), Silvestre Reyes (D-Tx 16), Cliff Stearns (R-Fl 3), Jean Schmidt (R-Oh 2) and John Sullivan (R-Ok 1). All their victors went on to win and hold the seat for the party in November.

As a result of the general election the Republicans remained the majority party but with fewer seats. The party balance before the election was 242 Republicans and 193 Democrats and the new House is made up of 234 Republicans and 201 Democrats, an overall gain of 8 seats for the Democrats. Of the 10 Democrat incumbents who lost, 4 lost to fellow incumbents. Of the 17 Republican incumbents who lost, 11 were first elected in 2010. At the other end of the scale was Roscoe Bartlett, a 10-term House member from Maryland and sub-committee chairman who lost his race to Democrat John Delaney by 20 percentage points. In the 22 open seats where no incumbent was running, each party won 11 races. Thus with Democrats controlling the Senate and Republicans controlling the House, we are in for at least two more years of divided political control on Capitol Hill, making President Obama's task all the harder.

Questions

1 Using the data in Tables 6.5 and 7.1, work out how many senators were elected in states won by the opposing party in the presidential race. What conclusion does one draw from this?
2 Why was the outcome of the Senate elections something of a surprise?
3 Why were there two incumbents in the same race in some House races?

Chapter 8

The Supreme Court, 2011–12

What you need to know

- The Supreme Court is the highest federal court in the USA.
- The Court is made up of nine justices, appointed by the president, for life.
- Of the nine justices who served in the term we consider in this chapter, five were appointed by Republican presidents and four by Democrats.
- The Supreme Court has the power of judicial review. This is the power to declare acts of Congress or actions of the executive branch — or acts or actions of state governments — unconstitutional, and thereby null and void.
- By this power of judicial review, the Court acts as the umpire of the Constitution and plays a leading role in safeguarding Americans' rights and liberties.
- In its most important judgement of the 2011–12 term, the Court would decide whether or not President Obama's healthcare reform — known as the Affordable Care Act (ACA) — was constitutional.
- The most controversial part of that legislation concerned the 'individual mandate' which requires (mandates) every (individual) American to buy health insurance if they are not covered by a government- or work-provided scheme.

Sometimes the Supreme Court passes an entire term — from October to June — without handing down any landmark decisions at all. Such was the previous term of 2010–11 (see Chapter 7, *US Government & Politics Annual Update 2012*). But the term which ended in June 2012 certainly had a blockbuster or two with the Court's decisions on President Obama's healthcare reforms and Arizona's immigration law likely to be talked about for decades to come (Table 8.1). It was also the first term since 2008–09 when the membership of the Court remained the same. The Court seems to go through periods of stability and change with regard to its membership. Having had no changes at all between 1994 and 2005, the Court then saw four new justices join the bench in 5 years — Chief Justice John Roberts in 2005, followed by associate justices Samuel Alito (2006), Sonia Sotomayor (2009) and Elena Kagan (2010). It often takes the justices a year or two to settle into their new role on the highest court in the land and also for relationships to develop between the nine members of the Court.

Table 8.1 Significant Supreme Court decisions, 2011–12 term

Case	Concerning	Decision
National Federation of Independent Businesses (NFIB) v *Sebelius*	Healthcare: individual mandate and expansion of Medicaid	5–4
Arizona v *United States*	Arizona immigration law	5–3
Jackson v *Hobbs* and *Miller* v *Alabama*	Mandatory life sentences without parole for juvenile murderers	5–4
American Tradition Partnership v *Bullock*	Ban on corporate political money	5–4
United States v *Alvarez*	Freedom of speech	6–3

Healthcare reform

Here was a decision of the Supreme Court which will rank alongside *Brown* v *Board of Education of Topeka* (1954), *Roe* v *Wade* (1973) and *Bush* v *Gore* (2000). It was truly a landmark decision. At exactly ten o'clock on the morning of Thursday 28 June 2012, Chief Justice John Roberts was the first to appear from behind the thick red curtains, followed by his eight colleagues to take their places in the black leather chairs in order of Court seniority, from the centre outwards. 'I have the opinion in *NFIB* v *Sebelius*,' the chief justice announced nonchalantly as if he had absolutely no idea why the court room was so packed on this particular morning.

Chief Justice Roberts spent the next quarter-of-an-hour reading what sounded like a political science lecture on the benefits of federalism before setting out the views of those who argued that the Affordable Care Act (ACA) was unconstitutional. The Fox News channel quickly decided what it thought Roberts had decided. An on-screen graphic read 'Supreme Court Finds Health Care Individual Mandate Unconstitutional.' CNN agreed, announcing that this part of the ACA had been found to be unconstitutional and therefore struck down by Roberts and the Court's conservative wing.

But having laid out the case why the Act might be unconstitutional, the chief justice spoke two words that neither Fox News nor CNN — nor quite a few Court-watchers — were expecting. 'We disagree.' We? It suddenly became clear for the first time that Chief Justice Roberts was not reading the majority opinion on behalf of himself and his fellow conservatives, but on behalf of himself and the liberal wing of the Court. 'We' constituted the chief justice along with justices Ginsburg, Breyer, Sotomayor and Kagan — the Clinton and Obama appointees. From one perspective, this was Pearl Harbor and 9/11 rolled into one; from another, it was a piece of masterly judicial statesmanship by the chief justice. For, as we shall see, in the way that he upheld 'Obamacare', Chief Justice Roberts enhanced the

reputation of the Court and of himself, and just for good measure laid down some important principles which are dear to the hearts of the conservatives he had on this day apparently deserted.

While passing the ACA in 2010, President Obama and congressional Democrats had argued that Congress could mandate every American to obtain healthcare insurance or pay a penalty under Congress's power 'to regulate Commerce among the several states' (Article I, Section 8, Clause 3). But Chief Justice Roberts disagreed:

> The power to *regulate* commerce presupposes the existence of commercial activity to be regulated...The individual mandate, however, does not regulate existing commercial activity. It instead compels individuals to *become* active in commerce by purchasing a product, on the grounds that their failure to do so affects interstate commerce...The Framers [of the Constitution] knew the difference between doing something and doing nothing. They gave Congress the power to *regulate* commerce, not to *compel* it. Ignoring that distinction would undermine the principle that the Federal Government is a government of limited and enumerated powers. The individual mandate thus cannot be sustained under Congress's power to 'regulate Commerce'.

Doubtless it was hearing that argument from Chief Justice Roberts that led some news outlets to the erroneous conclusion that Roberts was about to declare the individual mandate unconstitutional. But just as Chief Justice John Marshall in the landmark decision of *Marbury* v *Madison* (1803) had a judicial rabbit to pull out of his robes — so to speak — so did Chief Justice John Roberts in this case.

One might summarise the next step in Roberts's argument by asking, 'When is a mandate not a mandate?' Answer: 'When it's a tax.' For what Roberts argued was this: that the penalty that someone would pay if they refused to buy health insurance is not a mandate but a tax — paid to the Internal Revenue Service — that Congress *may* impose in accordance with the power vested in it by the opening ten words of Article I Section 8 that 'the Congress shall have Power to lay and collect taxes'. Therefore, stated Roberts, 'Our precedent demonstrates that Congress had the power to impose the [penalty for not purchasing health insurance] under the taxing power and that [this penalty] need not be read to do more than impose a tax. That is sufficient to sustain it.' Tucked away in a footnote on page 44 of the opinion was this simple explanation:

> Those subject to the individual mandate may lawfully forgo health insurance and pay higher taxes, or buy health insurance and pay lower taxes. The only thing that they may not lawfully do is not buy health insurance and not pay the resulting tax.

Game, set and match to the chief justice, and to justices Ginsburg, Breyer, Sotomayor and Kagan. These latter four thought the mandate was constitutional under the Commerce Clause, but they were happy to meet the chief justice halfway and agree it was also fine as a tax.

Chief Justice Roberts would be vilified for this decision by his usual conservative admirers in the media and in Congress, but like it or not, Roberts had pulled off a brilliant piece of judicial statecraft based upon good conservative principles — limiting the reach of the federal government, a narrow reading of the Commerce Clause and respect for precedent. And he had based it all on a principle established by his great hero, the much-revered Oliver Wendell Holmes, Jr. — associate justice of the Supreme Court from 1902 to 1932. Now Roberts's critics will allege his argument to be faulty because Congress never claimed the 'penalty' was a 'tax' — the Act calls it a 'penalty'. But here is Roberts quoting Holmes to justify his own reasoning:

> The text of a statute can sometimes have more than one possible meaning. And it is well established that if a statute has two possible meanings, one of which violates the Constitution, courts should adopt the meaning that does not do so. Justice Story said that 180 years ago…[and] Justice Holmes made the same point a century later: 'The rule is settled that as between two possible interpretations of a statute, by one of which it would be unconstitutional and the other it would be valid, our plain duty is to adopt that which will save the Act.'

So what did the dissenting minority say? 'We would find the Act invalid in its entirety,' wrote Justice Kennedy. The dissenting quartet of justices Kennedy, Scalia, Thomas and Alito claimed the Act was unconstitutional in its entirety because it could not be justified under Congress's power to regulate interstate commerce and that reclassifying the individual mandate's 'penalty' as a 'tax' was not constitutional interpretation but rather judges rewriting legislation, therefore a worrying example of judicial activism.

That left only the matter relating to the expansion of Medicaid under the Act to be resolved. Here the Court was split 7–2, with the chief justice siding with the Court's conservative wing, joined by justices Anthony Kennedy, Stephen Breyer and Elena Kagan. In their majority opinion, the Court upheld the major expansion of Medicaid by the ACA but limited the power of the federal government to enforce its provision by penalising states that refused to go along with it. Chief Justice Roberts said that the federal government could not compel states to comply by cutting off all federal money they receive for existing Medicaid programmes — aid that amounts to more than 10% of state budgets. The threatened loss of such federal money, according to Roberts, amounted to 'economic dragooning that leaves the states with no real option but to acquiesce in the Medicaid expansion'. It would be fine, said Roberts, for Congress to offer *extra* money to those states who comply but 'what Congress is not free to do is to penalise states that choose not to participate in that new programme by taking away their existing Medicaid funding'. Only justices Ginsburg and Sotomayor dissented from this part of the opinion.

Impact of the Court's decision
Altogether this was a remarkable judgement, a triumph for the President, congressional Democrats and the Supreme Court as a whole. In simple terms, it

was a mostly liberal decision based on mostly conservative principles and, given the major parties' symbols, maybe therefore a kind of pantomime horse with a donkey at the front and an elephant at the rear. But maybe the biggest winner in the long term was Chief Justice Roberts himself. Here's how Michael Gerson of the *Washington Post* summed up the decision on *The Newshour* on PBS the day after the decision:

> The decision itself was a wonder. It balanced so many interests. It was like juggling on a tightrope and [Chief Justice Roberts] did it very successfully [and it] really marked the emergence of Roberts as the key figure on the Court. He both avoided a major political crisis, gave conservatives things they wanted by restricting the Commerce Clause as it applies in these cases, and established himself as the central thinker on the Court. That's quite an achievement.

At his Senate confirmation hearings in September 2005, John Roberts had talked about the way he saw the role of a judge:

> Judges and [Supreme Court] justices are servants of the law. They are like umpires. Umpires don't make the rules; they apply them. They make sure everybody plays by the rules. But it is a limited role. Nobody ever went to a ball game to see the umpire.

Even those who were not initially minded to support Roberts's nomination liked what they heard. But many have wondered since whether Roberts's tenure as chief justice has lived up to those high ideals over the last 7 years. But in this judgement, Chief Justice Roberts showed more than glimpses of that limited, umpiring role. 'Our permissive reading of these powers is explained in part by a general reticence to invalidate the acts of the Nation's elected leaders,' stated Roberts in the majority opinion, backing this view with a quotation from an 1883 judgement of the Court, *United States* v *Harris*: '"Proper respect for a coordinate branch of the government", requires that we strike down an Act of Congress only if "the lack of constitutional authority to pass the Act in question is clearly demonstrated."' Roberts continued:

> Members of this Court are vested with the authority to interpret the law; we possess neither the expertise nor the prerogative to make policy judgements. Those decisions are entrusted to our Nation's leaders, who can be thrown out of office if the people disagree with them. It is not our job to protect the people from the consequences of their political choices.

In other words, 'Don't blame me, or this Court, for this healthcare law. We are here to make judicial decisions, not policy judgements. You elected President Obama and a Democratic Congress in 2008 who were promising healthcare reform. We're not sorting out this mess for you. You sort it out yourselves — at the ballot box. That's what elections are for.' Chief Justice Roberts had re-found his umpiring hat, or as Dana Milbank headlined it in the *Washington Post* the day after the decision was announced, 'The umpire strikes back'. And as David Von Drehle commented in an admiring cover story piece in *Time* magazine ('Roberts rules', 29 June 2012), 'Not since King Solomon offered to split the baby has a judge engineered a slicker solution to a bitterly divisive dispute.'

Other significant decisions

In *Arizona* v *United States*, the Court struck down three provisions of a controversial Arizona immigration law. Much like the healthcare decision this judgement also centred on the role of the federal government. Opponents of the law claimed that Arizona had encroached on areas of federal government authority in the regulation of immigration. In a 5–3 decision — Justice Kagan recused herself because of previous involvement in the case while serving as solicitor general — the Court struck down three of the law's major provisions because they either encroached on areas of exclusive federal government authority or interfered with federal government powers. Thus the Court struck down sections of the law which made it a crime to be in Arizona without legal papers or to apply for or get a job in the state. Justices Scalia, Thomas and Alito dissented. Here again was Chief Justice Roberts joining the Court's liberal wing.

In *Jackson* v *Hobbs* and *Miller* v *Alabama*, the Court ruled by 5 votes to 4 that a mandatory life sentence without chance of parole when given to a juvenile murderer infringed the provision of the 8th Amendment which forbids 'cruel and unusual punishments'. In this case, the four liberal justices were joined by Justice Kennedy, with the four conservative justices in the minority. This ruling was seen as an extension of the Court's 2005 decision in *Roper* v *Simmons* in which the Court had struck down the death penalty for juvenile murderers as unconstitutional on the same basis.

In *American Tradition Partnership* v *Bullock*, the Court reaffirmed its highly controversial *Citizens United* v *Federal Election Commission* (2010) decision concerning corporate campaign spending by extending it to state elections. The Court overturned a decision of the Montana Supreme Court which had upheld a 1912 state law banning corporate spending in Montana state elections. In another 5–4 decision, Justice Kennedy voted with the four conservatives, leaving the Court's four liberal justices in the minority — exactly the same voting pattern as in the 2010 decision.

A classic example of the Supreme Court's power to declare an Act of Congress unconstitutional, and thereby null and void, came this term in the case of *United States* v *Alvarez*. In 2006, Congress had unanimously passed the Stolen Valor Act to make it an offence to lie about the holding of military awards for bravery, and President Bush signed it into law in December of that year. But now the Supreme Court by 6 votes to 3 declared the law unconstitutional as it infringed the 1st Amendment guarantee of the right to freedom of speech. The Court's liberal quartet was again joined by Chief Justice Roberts and Justice Kennedy, leaving justices Scalia, Thomas and Alito as the dissenting minority.

Court statistics

In the 2011–12 term, the Court delivered 75 opinions (Table 8.2), fewer than the 80 (2010–11) and 86 (2009–10) in the two previous terms. Of these 75 opinions, 15 (20%) were 5–4 decisions, exactly the same percentage as in the previous term. In 10 of these 15 decisions (67%), the Court's four conservative justices (Roberts, Scalia, Thomas and Alito) were on one side and the four liberal justices (Ginsburg, Breyer, Sotomayor and Kagan) were on the other. In five of these decisions Justice Kennedy sided with the conservatives, including *American Tradition Partnership* v *Bullock*, and in five he sided with the liberals including *Miller* v *Alabama*. The justice most often in the majority on 5–4 decisions was yet again Justice Kennedy — the eighth consecutive term in which Justice Kennedy has held that distinction either jointly or solely. However, Kennedy was not in the majority on the most significant 5–4 decision of the term — the one concerning the Affordable Care Act. Justice Ginsburg was the justice least often in the majority in 5–4 decisions — the second term in three that she had held that spot. But then she *was* in the majority on the healthcare decision. Kennedy and Ginsburg also held the record for the justice most frequently in the majority and the minority respectively in all 75 decisions.

Table 8.2 Supreme Court statistics, 2006–12

Term	2006–07	2007–08	2008–09	2009–10	2010–11	2011–12
Number of decisions	68	67	74	86	80	75
% which were 5–4 decisions	33%	17%	31%	19%	20%	20%
Justice(s) most in majority in 5–4 decisions	Kennedy	Kennedy Thomas	Kennedy	Kennedy Thomas Scalia	Kennedy	Kennedy
Justice(s) most in minority in 5–4 decisions	Stevens	Breyer	Breyer	Ginsburg	Breyer	Ginsburg
% which conservatives won 5–4 decisions	54%	33%	48%	50%	63%	42%
% which liberals won 5–4 decisions	25%	33%	22%	19%	25%	42%
Two justices most in agreement	Roberts Alito	Roberts Scalia	Roberts Alito	Ginsburg Sotomayor	Roberts Alito	Scalia Thomas
Two justices most in disagreement	Thomas Stevens	Thomas Stevens	Thomas Stevens	Thomas Stevens	Alito Ginsburg	Scalia Ginsburg
Justice(s) most in the majority	Kennedy	Roberts	Kennedy	Kennedy Roberts	Kennedy	Kennedy
Justice(s) most in the minority	Stevens	Thomas	Stevens	Stevens	Ginsburg	Ginsburg

The two justices most often in agreement were Antonin Scalia and Clarence Thomas who agreed in 93% of cases, just beating John Roberts and Samuel Alito — last year's winners in this category — who agreed in 91% of cases. One possible point of significance was that the two Obama appointees — Sonia Sotomayor and Elena Kagan — who had agreed on 94% of cases in 2010–11, agreed in just 84% of cases in 2011–12. And they disagreed over the Medicare provision in *NFIB* v *Sebelius*. This year, Kagan's voting record was more like that of Clinton appointee Stephen Breyer, while Sotomayor's was more like that of the other Clinton appointee Ruth Bader Ginsburg. This might suggest that of the two Obama appointees, Sotomayor may prove to be the justice with the more reliably liberal voting record. The two justices most at odds with one another were Antonin Scalia and Ruth Bader Ginsburg — another piece of evidence which suggests that Justice Ginsburg is now the most reliably liberal member of the current Court following the retirement in 2010 of John Paul Stevens. Scalia and Ginsburg were on opposite sides in 79% of all non-unanimous cases and in 93% of 5–4 decisions.

The justice who authored the most majority opinions during this term was Anthony Kennedy with nine, including four of the 5–4 decisions — a likely statistic for the justice most often in the majority. Those authoring the most dissenting opinions were Scalia and Breyer with ten each, whereas Kennedy authored only two dissents, one being the healthcare minority opinion.

Conclusion

Interviewed on *Piers Morgan Tonight* in July 2012, Justice Antonin Scalia remarked that 'the Supreme Court is not a political institution', adding that 'I don't think any of my colleagues on any case vote the way they do for political reasons'. In one sense Scalia is of course right. The Supreme Court is not a political institution manned by politicians, it is a judicial institution manned by judges. But its members are appointed by a politician and confirmed by politicians, and it makes decisions that have significant political repercussions as this Court's term clearly showed.

Questions

1 What was so surprising about the make-up of the five-member majority in the *NFIB* v *Sebelius* decision on the Affordable Care Act?
2 What is the 'individual mandate' in the Affordable Care Act?
3 Summarise Chief Justice Roberts's argument as to why the Act's individual mandate could not be justified by the Constitution's Commerce Clause.
4 How did Roberts justify the individual mandate?
5 Explain the quotation from Oliver Wendell Holmes.
6 What was the view of the seven-member majority regarding the Act's Medicaid provision?
7 What did Roberts mean when he said, 'It is not our job to protect the people from the consequences of their political choices'?
8 What did the Court decide in the case of *Arizona* v *United States*? Who made up the five-member majority in this case?
9 Analyse the data presented in Table 8.2, especially in the right-hand column.
10 Do you agree with Justice Scalia that 'the Supreme Court is not a political institution'? Justify your answer.